Editor
Walter Kelly

Editorial Project Manager
Karen J. Goldfluss, M.S. Ed.

Editor in Chief
Sharon Coan, M.S. Ed.

Creative Director
Elayne Roberts

Associate Designer
Denise Bauer

Cover Artist
Denise Bauer

Product Manager
Phil Garcia

Imaging
James Edward Grace
Ralph Olmedo, Jr.

Publishers
Rachelle Cracchiolo, M.S. Ed.
Mary Dupuy Smith, M.S. Ed.

Teacher's Guide to Reading and Language Skills

Author

Donna M. Miller

Teacher Created Materials, Inc.
6421 Industry Way
Westminster, CA 92683
www.teachercreated.com
ISBN-1-55734-023-4
©1998 Teacher Created Materials, Inc.
Reprinted, 1999
Made in U.S.A.

Table of Contents

Introduction

Children's literature books offer a wealth of opportunities as valid instructional tools to meaningfully teach the basic reading and language arts skills to students. Learners use the reading skills during reading; therefore, examples of the skills can be found in what a child reads.

This handbook grew out of the desire to use children's literature books to teach and reinforce basic reading and language arts skills. A study was conducted of basic reading and language arts skills and objectives, a current course of study (reading and language arts only), and many children's literature books. Each book was read and evaluated according to useability as an instructional tool. The books and skills were then matched. Many of the books listed are also accompanied by a brief example of how the skills can be taught using that specific book.

Literature has been communicated by these four components of our language.

Many other skills can be reinforced by each volume listed in this resource book. Each time we expose children to a literature book, we are also exposing them to many opportunities to experience, analyze, and communicate about the book.

How to Use This Book

This book has been designed as a helpful tool for educators desiring to teach skills through the use of authentic children's literature books.

Included in this book are the following sections:

Index of Skills
These pages list specific skills necessary to successfully meet reading and language objectives.

Sample Lessons
Five sample lesson plans are provided. These may be used as models for planning your skill lessons. A blank, two-page reproducible lesson plan form is located in the management section. Use the blank form to develop each skill lesson that accompanies your literature choice.

Skills and Literature Connections
This section features each skill with its accompanying literature.
(Even though the reading and language skills are often intertwined and interchanged, this book has been divided into these two sections for ease of location of skills.)

Management
A Lesson Plan Form, Skills Checklist, and Additional Literature Appendix form are located in this section.

Children's Literature References
In this section you will find publishing information for the books used in this unit.

To introduce or reinforce a specific skill, follow these steps:

1. Locate the skill in the Index of Skills. A comprehensive list of reading and language skills is provided on pages 5–8.

2. Turn to the page(s) of the Skills and Literature Connections section where the skill is listed. Several books which exemplify or reinforce the skill are listed below each skill section. Many of the books also contain brief descriptions of how the book matches the skill.

3. Reproduce and fill out the Lesson Plan Form on pages 69 and 70. It is suggested that you read one or more books from the section to your students. Extension or follow-up activities are recommended to enrich each lesson. Children need many examples and much "think time" to thoroughly process a skill. Various forms of application are also recommended so that the children can internalize the skill.

For recordkeeping purposes, a reproducible Skills Checklist form is provided on pages 71–78. Upon completion of a skill, check off the appropriate skill and note any significant information on the form. A reproducible form is provided on page 79 to allow you to personalize your handbook by adding books that reinforce the skill in this unit.

Index of Skills

Note: Throughout this book, skills will be referred to by letter and number identification. Skills with the letter **R** represent the **reading objectives**; skills with the letter **L** represent the **language objectives**.

Skill	Description of Skills
R 1	identifying words that rhyme
R 2	developing eye, motor, and voice control
R 3	identifying a detail
R 4	making inferences
R 5	developing a sense of reading enjoyment
R 6	reading Dolch words
R 7	reading second grade Thorndike words
R 8	using words correctly in oral sentences
R 9	using words correctly in written sentences
R 10	recognizing meanings of words in context
R 11	identifying some foreign words
R 12	using figurative language in written and oral work
R 13	using formal and informal language at appropriate times
R 14	identifying synonyms
R 15	identifying antonyms
R 16	identifying homophones, given two definitions
R 17	using the context of illustrations to define a word
R 18	using direct explanation to define a word
R 19	using experience to define a word
R 20	using mode or tone of voice
R 21	using an example to define a word
R 22	comparing irregular plural nouns to singular nouns
R 23	listening to and reproducing sounds
R 24	listening to and identifying similar and different sounds
R 25	identifying syllables heard in written and oral words
R 26	matching consonant sounds
R 27	matching consonant blends and digraphs
R 28	matching vowels and vowel sounds

Index of Skills *(cont.)*

Skill	Description of Skills
R 29	sounding out words beginning with consonant blends and digraphs
R 30	sounding out one-syllable words with long vowel sounds
R 31	sounding out one-syllable words with short vowel sounds
R 32	sounding out one-syllable words with vowel combinations
R 33	sounding out one-syllable words with digraphs
R 34	building and using new words by using the same ending
R 35	reading words with same ending sounds
R 36	identifying prefix, suffix, and root words in affixed words
R 37	reading and building compound words
R 38	reading and building contractions—apostrophe usage
R 39	reading possessives—singular, plural, and apostrophe usage
R 40	following stated directions
R 41	recalling stated details
R 42	identifying stated causes and effects in written material
R 43	drawing conclusions implied in reading passages
R 44	comparing and contrasting ideas in reading selections
R 45	stating a simplified analysis of a character in a story
R 46	demonstrating empathy with characters in a story
R 47	summarizing a written passage
R 48	stating the main idea in a written passage
R 49	applying previously learned information to a new situation
R 50	distinguishing facts from opinions in a story
R 51	orally reading and interpreting sentences, using punctuation and phrasing
R 52	demonstrating comprehension of material read silently
R 53	identifying the stated main idea heard in a story
R 54	recalling stated sequential events heard in a story
R 55	selecting critical details heard in a story
R 56	listening to and reading fiction stories
R 57	listening to and reading nonfiction stories
R 58	listening to and reading poetry

Index of Skills *(cont.)*

Skill	Description of Skills
L 1	recognizing singular and plural nouns
L 2	recognizing regular verbs in the present, past, and future tenses
L 3	recognizing and using subject-verb agreement
L 4	recognizing singular and plural personal pronouns
L 5	recognizing polite pronoun order
L 6	recognizing double negatives
L 7	capitalizing the first word of a sentence
L 8	capitalizing proper nouns
L 9	capitalizing days of the week and months of the year
L 10	capitalizing holidays
L 11	capitalizing the personal pronoun *I*
L 12	capitalizing titles before proper names
L 13	capitalizing initials of persons' names
L 14	capitalizing parts of addresses
L 15	using periods after declarative and imperative sentences
L 16	using periods after numbers, initials, and abbreviations
L 17	using commas to separate items in addresses
L 18	using commas to separate items when writing the date
L 19	using commas after the greeting and closing in personal letters
L 20	using a question mark after an interrogative sentence
L 21	using an exclamation point at the end of an exclamatory sentence
L 22	writing a sentence using a simple subject and verb
L 23	writing a sentence with agreement of subject and verb
L 24	identifying the topic sentence of a paragraph
L 25	writing a short creative composition
L 26	writing poetry
L 27	identifying heading, greeting, body, closing, and signature of a letter; arranging a letter neatly
L 28	identifying the return address on an envelope; writing a block-style address on an envelope
L 29	recognizing and using wordless picture books
L 30	recognizing and using creative dramatics
L 31	recognizing and using nursery rhymes

Index of Skills *(cont.)*

Skill	Description of Skills
L 32	recognizing song
L 33	recognizing rhyming endings in poetry
L 34	distinguishing between casual and attentive listening
L 35	listening for the main idea
L 36	listening for details
L 37	listening for sequence
L 38	listening for cause and effect
L 39	listening for fact and opinion
L 40	understanding listening for entertainment
L 41	understanding that listening is a part of communication
L 42	using good eye contact
L 43	being aware of body language
L 44	concentrating while listening
L 45	summarizing what has been listened to
L 46	visualizing what has been listened to
L 47	locating and identifying spelling patterns
L 48	identifying and using r-controlled vowels
L 49	identifying vowel-consonant patterns
L 50	identifying and locating guide words and entry words
L 51	locating and using illustrations
L 52	translating a story into pictures
L 53	interpreting meanings of collages
L 54	locating glossary, guide words, title page, table of contents, titles and subtitles, and chapter headings
L 55	alphabetizing words to the first letter
L 56	skimming for information
L 57	being aware of a dictionary's use
L 58	being able to read and use simple graphs, maps, and charts

#023 Teacher's Guide to Reading and Language Skills　　8

Sample Lessons

Lesson Plan #1

Resources

Poem: "Nine Mice"
Book: A New Kid on the Block
Author: Jack Prelutsky

Skill(s)/Objective(s)

The student will be able to identify various vowel/consonant spelling patterns of words with a long /i/ sound. (See page_____.)

Procedure

1. Chorally read poem together several times, establishing a rhythm to the reading.
2. Have the students use context clues to guess meanings of unfamiliar words.
3. Introduce (or review) long /i/ vowel sound. Slowly read the poem. Have students raise their hands when they hear a word with a long /i/ sound.
4. Have the students take turns finding words from the poem with a long /i/ sound. Write the words on the chalkboard or chart paper as students identify them.
5. Have the students observe the list of long /i/ words. Ask the students to group them according to spelling patterns.

Application

Have the students look through another poem or a story that they are currently reading to find words with a long /i/ sound. The students can work independently or with a partner to sort their lists by spelling patterns.

Notes/Comments

Place long /i/ pattern cards and activity cards in learning center for students to review.

Sample Lessons *(cont.)*

Lesson Plan #2

Resources

Book: <u>The Little House</u>
Author: Virginia Lee Burton

Skill(s)/Objective(s)

The students will be able to compare and contrast country and city living.
(See page_____.)

Procedure

1. Read story orally to students. Discuss.
2. Draw a Venn diagram on chalkboard or chart paper. Label the two parts of the diagram CITY and COUNTRY.
3. Read the story again, stopping after every two pages. Have the children give specific details that tell about living in the city or the country. List these under the appropriate headings on the Venn diagram.
4. Have the students suggest ways that city living and country living are similar. List these in the center overlapping part of the Venn diagram.

Application

The students can draw pictures showing the differences between city and country living.

Have the students present their pictures to the class.

The students can work alone or in small groups to make a Venn diagram showing the differences in housing between the city and the country.

Notes/Comments

Prepare a bulletin board on which to display the students' city and country pictures.

Sample Lessons *(cont.)*

Lesson Plan #3

Resources

Book: <u>A House Is a House for Me</u>
Author: Mary Ann Hoberman

Skill(s)/Objective(s)

The students will be able to make inferences as to which items are houses for the other items. (See page____.)

Procedure

1. Read half the book to the students to establish a pattern of thinking.

2. Discuss how a cookie could be a "house" for chocolate chips. Discuss other examples until the children are able to easily verbalize their thinking.

3. Now read the rest of the book slowly, one verse at a time. This time leave out the word that tells what the house is for. Have the children supply possibilities. Discuss how more than one possibility could make sense.

Application

Give each student a sentence about an item being a "house" for something else. Leave a blank for the student to fill in a word that makes sense.
Have each child illustrate his/her sentence. Collect all the drawings to compile into a class book.
Example: A glass is a house for milk.

Notes/Comments

Create extensions of this activity that give practice in letting the students infer or perceive elements that contain or are "houses" for other elements.

Sample Lessons *(cont.)*

Lesson Plan #4

Resources

Book: <u>The Year at Maple Hill Farm</u>
Author: Alice and Martin Provensen

Skill(s)/Objective(s)

The student will be able to capitalize the months of the year correctly.

Procedure

1. Read the story to the students.
2. Ask the children to tell what is different about each page. (Question them to direct their thinking and elicit responses that each page depicts a different month of the year.)
3. Have the students note that the name of each month is capitalized on each page spread.

Application

Have each child create a minibook entitled "The Year at_____'s House." On each page the student will illustrate a picture showing something that the child (or child's family) does during each month. Care is to be taken in forming the capital letters for each month.

The pages will be in consecutive order from January through December. Along with each illustration have children write a sentence beginning with "In" and the name of the month, as in example below. Example: In January my family and I like to make snowmen.

Notes/Comments

Display minibooks on a library table in the room for sharing with others. Afterward, the minibooks can be taken home to serve as personalized calendars for each student's family.

Sample Lessons *(cont.)*

Lesson Plan #5

Resources
Book: <u>Harold and the Purple Crayon</u>
Author: Crockett Johnson

Skill(s)/Objective(s)
The student will be able to translate a story into pictures.

Procedures
1. Read the story to the children.
2. Discuss how Harold solved his problem each time (he drew a picture with a purple crayon of what would solve the problem).
3. Reread the story, stopping at each point where Harold encounters a problem. Have the students orally brainstorm other possible solutions to each problem.

Application
Have the students choose one of the problems that Harold encountered and use a purple crayon to draw a different solution.
Have the students share their illustrations with large or small groups.
Encourage the children to share the solutions their drawings show.
Create a purple bulletin board on which to display the purple solutions. Title it "Purple Problems—Purple Solutions."

Notes/Comments
Extend the skill by creating whole stories into a series of pictures.

Auditory Perception

Skill R 1: identifying words that rhyme

❏ *Better Not Get Wet, Jesse Bear*
Author: Nancy White Carlstrom
This end-rhyme story tells of Jesse's attempts to get wet, but Mother or Father Bear is always there to warn him not to get wet.

❏ *Hi Bears, Bye Bears*
Author: Niki Yektai
The rhyming words in this book are not at the ends of the lines; they are the next-to-the-last words. Example: soft bear, rich bear, poor bear, witch bear. The illustrations match the text very well to give clues to emergent or nonreaders.

❏ *Into the Night*
Author: Deborah Heiligman
Every other ending word in each line rhymes in this story about exploring outside.

❏ *Jake Baked the Cake*
Author: B. G. Hennessy
The rhymes in the text of this story about preparing for a wedding occur within each line itself. Example: Mr. Fine painted the sign.

❏ *Jamberry*
Author: Bruce Degen
Each of the rhyming words in this book ends with the word *berry*.

❏ *Madeline*
Author: Ludwig Bemelmans
The story of a small girl, her friends, and an appendectomy is told in end-line rhyme.

❏ *Mitten/Kitten*
Author: Jerome Martin
As the page is turned, a new illustration with the item name is shown using part of the original illustration and text.

❏ *One Fish, Two Fish, Red Fish, Blue Fish*
Author: Dr. Seuss
Many rhyming words are presented throughout this book in both text and illustrations.

Auditory Perception *(cont.)*

Skill R 1: identifying words that rhyme *(cont.)*

❏ *One Hungry Monster*
Author: Bruce McMillan
This book combines rhyming with counting.

❏ *One Sun*
Author: Bruce McMillan
This book of terse verse (two monosyllabic words that sound alike) uses photographs to present each set of rhymes.

❏ *Pig in a Barrow*
Author: Bert Kitchen
A different animal is featured on each page with the end-line text rhymes and the illustrations working together to convey meaning.

❏ *The Wonderful Pigs of Jillian Jiggs*
Author: Phoebe Gilman
The end rhymes in this book have irregular spelling patterns. Examples: warning/morning, eyelashes/mustaches, galore/floor.

Kinesthetic Development

Skill R 2: developing eye, motor, and voice control

❏ *Christopher Columbus—A Punch and Play Storybook*
As children read this story, they can manipulate the figures and items mentioned in the text to go along with the storyline. (motor control)

❏ *Demi's Find the Animal ABC*
Author: Demi
Eye control can be developed as children use this alphabet book to find featured animals hidden among many others. (eye control)

❏ *I Like to See—A Book About the Five Senses*
Author: Jean Tymms
After reading this book, children can feel, hear, taste, touch, and smell many things in their own environment. The results can then be discussed and written about. (motor control)

❏ *Round Trip*
Author: Ann Jonas
Read from front to back, this unusual book focuses on the black parts of the illustrations. The reader turns the book over, reads the story, and concentrates on the white parts of the illustrations. (eye control)

Kinesthetic Development *(cont.)*

Skill R 2: developing eye, motor, and voice control *(cont.)*

❑ *Something BIG Has Been Here*

Author: Jack Prelutsky
Poem: "Slow Sloth's Slow Song" (page 65)
Children can practice voice control while reading this poem very slowly. (voice control)

❑ *Something BIG Has Been Here*

Author: Jack Prelutsky
Poem: "There's No One as Slow as Slomona" (page 74)
This poem will allow children to read the words as they think Slomona would read them. (voice control)

❑ *The Trek*

Author: Ann Jonas
A girl's walk to school becomes a walk in the jungle as she imagines ordinary objects to be animals. Children will have to look carefully to see all the illustrations have to offer. (eye control)

Oral Comprehension and Interpretation

Skill R 3: identifying a detail

❑ *Best Friends for Frances*

Author: Russell Hoban
Frances states qualities for a best friend within the story. See if children can recall these qualities after hearing this story.

❑ *Cloudy with a Chance of Meatballs*

Author: Judi Barrett
Children can identify details about the town of Chewandswallow, where food falls from the sky each day.

❑ *If I Were a Penguin*

Author: Heidi Goennel
The reader is given a detail that makes each animal unique and a description of something that the animal can do because of this uniqueness.

❑ *Life in the Rainforest*

Author: Lucy Baker
This book includes many factual details about the rain forest for children to identify.

❑ *Princess Abigail and the Wonderful Hat*

Author: Steven Kroll
Many hats are described in this book about a king who wears hats instead of crowns. Children can identify details by stating and describing words about the hats or by stating events from the story.

Oral Comprehension and Interpretation *(cont.)*

Skill R 4: making inferences

❑ *Animals Sleeping*

Author: Masayuki Yabuuchi

The reader is asked to guess how each of the listed animals sleeps.

❑ *A House Is a House for Me*

Author: Many Ann Hoberman

This book explores "houses" for everyday items, such as "a cookie is a house for a chocolate chip." After reading half of the book to children to establish a pattern of thinking, leave out one item that has a "house." See if the children can guess which item is the "house."

❑ *Is Your Mama a Llama?*

Author: Deborah Guarino

Read the clues about each animal to the students. Have them guess which animal is being described.

❑ *Jonathan Cleaned Up—Then He Heard a Sound*

Author: Robert Munsch

This is a great book to read in portions, stopping frequently to have students predict what will happen next.

❑ *Look Again!*

Author: Tana Hoban

Portions of black and white photographs are revealed for the reader to guess what object is behind.

❑ *Look! Look! Look!*

Author: Tana Hoban

Everyday photographs of items are covered, with only small portions revealed. The reader makes inferences as to the identities of the items.

❑ *One Hunter*

Author: Pat Hutchins

Each page gives picture clues to animals found on the next page.

❑ *Q Is for Duck*

Authors: Mary Yielding and Michael Folsom

After reading several pages to the students, ask them to guess why each letter stands for the object stated.

Oral Comprehension and Interpretation *(cont.)*

Skill R 4: making inferences *(cont.)*

❑ *There's Something in My Attic*
Author: Mercer Mayer
Children will have fun guessing what is in the attic.

❑ *Which Way Hugo?*
Author: Morgan Matthews
Hugo's feet hurt because he is always running to get from one spot to another to eat. Have children come up with ways that Hugo could get his food without having his feet hurt from running.

❑ *Who's Hiding Here?*
Author: Yoshi
Various animals are hiding on the next page. The author states clues along with part of each page being cut out to help reveal the identity of the hidden animals.

❑ *Whose Footprints?*
Author: Masayuki Yabuuchi
The reader is shown a footprint and then asked to guess which animal made the footprint.

Skill R 5: developing a sense of reading enjoyment

The teacher may insert his or her own favorites here according to the interests of the class. The emphasis should be on just having fun reading and sharing books.

Sight

Skill R 6: reading Dolch words

The books listed below all contain many examples of Dolch words.

- *The Carrot Seed*
  Author: Ruth Krauss
- *Frog and Toad Are Friends*
  Author: Arnold Lobel
- *Happy Rhythms and Rhymes*
  Poem: "If I Were Small" (page 17)

Author: Patricia M. Cavanaugh
- *Mouse Soup*
  Author: Arnold Lobel
- *Sam and the Firefly*
  Author: P. D. Eastman

Skill R 7: reading second-grade Thorndike words

The books below contain many examples of the second-grade Thorndike words.

- *The Berenstain Bears on the Moon*
  Authors: Stan and Jan Berenstain
- *The Giving Tree*
  Author: Shel Silverstein
- *Go, Dog, Go*
  Author: P.D. Eastman
- *I'll Teach My Dog 100 Words*
  Author: Michael Frith

- *My First Book of Words—10,000 Words Every Child Should Know*
  Author: Scholastic Editors
- *Owl at Home*
  Author: Arnold Lobel

Word Meaning

Skill R 8: using words correctly in oral sentences

- *Something BIG Has Been Here*
  Poem: "A Remarkable Adventure" (page 56)
  Author: Jack Prelutsky
  After hearing this poem, the children should be able to use many of the words stated in the poem in oral sentences.

- *Growing Wild*
  Authors: Marilyn Bass and Marvin Goldman
  This book presents different types of plants, uses of the plants, and illustrations of the parts of plants. The parts of the plants are labeled for further understanding. Children can use the names of the parts of the plants in oral sentences.

- *If You Traveled West in a Covered Wagon*
  Author: Ellen Levine
  Many "west" words such as *covered wagon, prairie schooners, wagon train,* and *Continental Divide* are discussed in this book. Children can demonstrate understanding of these terms by using them correctly in oral sentences.

Word Meaning *(cont.)*

Skill R 8: using words correctly in oral sentences *(cont.)*

❑ *The Little Engine That Could*
Author: Watty Piper
See if children can use *passenger train, freight train, engine,* and *switching engine* correctly in oral sentences after hearing this story read aloud.

❑ *My First Book About Space*
Author: Dinah L. Moche
Many space-related words such as *gravity, star, constellations,* and *planets* are used in this book. Students can practice using these and other words correctly.

Skill R 9: using words correctly in written sentences

❑ *From Seed to Plant*
Author: Gail Gibbons
After reading this story, the students will correctly use the names of the parts of a plant in sentences along with a written description of each part of the plant.

❑ *Harry the Dirty Dog*
Author: Gene Zion
Illustrations and text give clues to many words, such as *coal chute, flip-flopped, furiously, dashed,* and *lovingly.* Have students use them in sentences or stories.

❑ *Our Wonderful Seasons*
Author: Elizabeth Marcus
Many terms related to the seasons appear here—*hemisphere, orbit, North Pole,* and *equator.* Children can practice these terms in written sentences or stories.

❑ *Two-Way Words*
Author: C. Imbior Kudrna
Multiple-meaning words are shown in an illustration with a simple definition listed. Illustrations and text work together to show meanings. Children can use this book as a model to define multiple-meaning words.

❑ *The Very Quiet Cricket*
Author: Eric Carle
Attributes of insects appear as the Very Quiet Cricket communicates with his friends. After this story, students can write the attributes of the insects.

Skill R 10: recognizing meanings of words in context

❑ *Always Room for One More*
Author: Sorche Nic Leodhas
This book tells an old Scottish tale. Some of the original Scottish words have been left in the story. Through the use of context, see if children can tell the meanings. A simple glossary of the Scottish words from the story is provided.

Sight (cont.)

Skill R 10: recognizing meanings of words in context (cont.)

❑ *Something BIG Has Been Here*
Poem: "My Mother Made a Meat Loaf" (page 66)
By: Jack Prelutsky
Words such as *unblemished, cleaver, flabbergasted, powerless,* and *trample* are used in context to give clues to the meanings of the words.

❑ *The Storm Book*
Author: Charlotte Zolotow
The illustrations and the text combine beautifully to give the meanings of many words associated with "storm."

❑ *Where the Wild Things Are*
Author: Maurice Sendak
Words such as *gnashed, tamed, rumpus,* and *private* are used in context and shown with the illustrations.

❑ *Wonders of the Forest*
Author: Francene Sabin
The text and the illustrations combine to give meaning to several forest words such as *canopy, understory, shrub layer, herb layer,* and *fungi.*

Skill R 11: identifying some foreign words

❑ *Nine Days to Christmas*
Authors: Marie Hall Ets and Aurora Labastida
This Spanish Christmas book guides the reader to understand not only Spanish Christmas traditions, but also some Spanish words associated with Christmas.

❑ *Song of the Swallows*
Author: Leo Politi
Spanish words are used throughout the text as Old Julian tells the story of the swallows coming to Capistrano.

❑ *Twenty-one Children Plus TEN*
Author: Virginia H. Ormsby
Twenty-one second graders are happy until 10 Spanish-speaking children are put into their class. Finally they all become friends. Spanish numbers from one to thirty-one are introduced.

Skill R 12: using figurative language in written and oral work

In both text and illustrations, the following books use figurative language.

❑ *A Chocolate Moose for Dinner*
Author: Fred Gwynne

❑ *A Little Pigeon Toad*
Author: Fred Gwynne

❑ *Amelia Bedelia and the Baby*
Amelia Bedelia Helps Out
Good Work, Amelia Bedelia
Author: Peggy Parish

Sight *(cont.)*

Skill R 12: using figurative language in written and oral work *(cont.)*

❑ *In a Pickle and Other Funny Idioms*
Author: Marvin Terban

❑ *The King Who Rained*
Author: Fred Gwynne

❑ *Morris Has a Cold*
Author: Bernard Wiseman

❑ *Rugs Have Naps (But Never Take Them)*
Author: Charles Klasky

Skill R 13: using formal and informal language at appropriate times

❑ *The Berenstain Bears Get in a Fight*

Authors: Stan and Jan Berenstain
Throughout the book proper ways to behave are discussed.

❑ *I Can Read About Good Manners*

Author: Erica Frost
Many "manners tips" are given in this book.

❑ *The Manners Book*

Author: June Behrens
A little boy encounters situations where manners or formal language are appropriate. He asks his teddy bear, Ned, what to do in each situation.

❑ *Mind Your Manners*

Author: Peggy Parish
This is a book using simple language to tell the reader the proper way to act.

Skill R 14: identifying synonyms

❑ *Alexander and the Terrible, Horrible, No Good, Very Bad Day*

Author: Judith Viorst
Throughout the book the phrase "*terrible, horrible, no good, very bad,*" appears, using synonyms to describe a bad day.

❑ *A Big Fish Story*

Authors: Joanne and David Wylie
This book uses synonyms for "big" to describe the catch of the day.

❑ *Something BIG Has Been Here*

Poem: "I Am Tired of Being Little" (page 24)
Author: Jack Prelutsky
Synonyms for both big and little are given in this poem.

❑ *Synonyms*   ❑ *More Synonyms*   ❑ *Still More Synonyms*

By: Joan Hanson
Synonyms are shown in the illustrations with each synonym labeled.

❑ *Teeny Tiny*

Author: Jill Bennett
After reading this book, discuss the synonyms in the title. If children understand the concept of synonyms, they should be able to give other synonyms for teeny and tiny.

Sight (cont.)

Skill R 14: identifying synonyms *(cont.)*

❏ *Ten Little Mice*

Author: Joyce Dunbar
This backwards counting sequential story uses many synonyms for *rush*, as each mouse finds a reason to go back to his or her nest.

Skill R 15: identifying antonyms

❏ *Antonyms*　　　　❏ *More Antonyms*　　　　❏ *Still More Antonyms*

Author: Joan Hanson
These books show opposite words with simple illustrations side by side.

❏ *Beginning to Learn About Opposites*

Author: Richard L. Allington
This book lists opposites side by side and tells why they are opposites.

❏ *Big Ones, Little Ones*

Author: Tana Hoban
Mother and baby animals are shown as opposites of big and little.

❏ *Exactly the Opposite*

Author: Tana Hoban
Opposites are shown throughout the book with photographs, not words.

❏ *Go, Dog, Go*

Author: P. D. Eastman
Many antonyms are humorously presented in both illustrations and text.

❏ *I Am*

Author: Rita Milios
This book is ideal for introducing antonyms. Each page has a simple illustration with a three-word sentence which relates to the opposites being introduced.

❏ *Something BIG Has Been Here*

Poem: "I Am Tired of Being Little" (page 24)
Author: Jack Prelutsky
Antonyms for *big* and *little* are introduced within the poem.

❏ *Old Hat, New Hat*

Authors: Stan and Jan Berenstain
Phrases about hats are presented in the form of opposites.

❏ *Paddington's Opposites*

Author: Michael Bond
Each page spread shows two pictures of Paddington Bear demonstrating a pair of opposites. The names of the opposites being presented accompany each illustration.

❏ *Push, Pull, Empty, Full*

Author: Tana Hoban
Antonyms are presented with photographs and words displayed side by side.

Sight (*cont.*)

Skill R 16: identifying homophones, given two definitions

❑ *A Little Pigeon Toad*   ❑ *A Chocolate Moose for Dinner*   ❑ *The King Who Rained*

Author: Fred Gwynne
Many of the figurative language examples presented in the above books use homophones to derive their meaning. A class lesson could include finding the homophone that would make the sentence literally correct. Example—"The king who rained" would become "The king who reigned."

❑ *Eight Ate—A Feast of Homonym Riddles*

Author: Marvin Terban
The text and illustrations combine to show the meanings of presented homonyms.

❑ *Homographs*

Author: Joan Hanson
Homographs are simply presented in text and illustrations in this book.

❑ *A New Treasury of Children's Poetry*

Poem: "One, Two, Three—Gough"
Editor: Joanna Cole
Homonyms are substituted for the meaningful words in this poem.

❑ *Which Witch Is Which?*

Author: Pat Hutchins
The author gives visual and written clues to tell the reader which witch is which.

Skill R 17: using the context of illustrations to define a word

❑ *A Dark, Dark Tale*

Author: Ruth Brown
Text and illustrations give the meanings of words such as *moor* and *cupboard*.

❑ *The Alphabet Tree*

Author: Leo Lionni
At the beginning of the story, letters are isolated in bushes and trees. A wind blows and mixes them up. The letters then combine to form words and sentences. The illustrations show this happening.

❑ *The Brementown Musicians*

Author: Debby Slier
This familiar story is written using rhebus style. The pictures within the sentences help to add to the meanings of words in the story.

❑ *Clifford's Word Book*

Author: Norman Bridwell
On each set of pages, the story continues with items labeled so that even nonreaders can "read" the words by identifying the pictures labeled around the page.

Sight (cont.)

Skill R 17: using the context of illustrations to define a word (cont.)

❏ *The Elephant's Child*

Author: Lisa Meltzer
This rebus story uses illustrations within the text to convey meaning.

❏ *From A to Z*

Authors: Irene and Hallie Coletta
Each page uses a combination of words and rebus pictures to describe a word beginning with a specific letter.

❏ *"I Can't," Said the Ant*

Author: Polly Cameron
Pictures of kitchen items are shown giving responses to the ant and the fallen teapot situation.

❏ *Miss Rumphius*

Author: Barbara Cooney
By reading the descriptions of the places Alice visited in her lifetime, students can use the context of the illustrations to gain meaning about the settings.

❏ *The Story of Vania*

Author: Helene Pons
Many sea- and boat-related words are used in this story. The illustrations help to show the meanings of many of these words.

Skill R 18: using direct explanation to define a word

❏ *The Bears' Vacation*

Authors: Stan and Jan Berenstain
This book gives valid water safety rules in a humorous way. After hearing the story, children can explain water safety rules.

❏ *The Biggest Bear*

Author: Lynd Ward
After hearing the story, the students can be asked to tell why the bear could not be kept as a pet.

❏ *The Doorbell Rang*

Author: Pat Hutchins
Use this story to see if the children can explain dividing.

❏ *The Empty Pot*

Author: Demi
This story can be used to see if the students can explain why Ping was honored.

❏ *What's Inside?*

Author: May Garelick
After reading this book, the children can explain how an egg is hatched.

Sight *(cont.)*

Skill R 19: using experience to define a word

❏ *Best Friends*
Author: Steven Kellogg
After hearing this story, children can use their own experiences and the information from the book to define "friends."

❏ *Chester's Way*
Author: Kevin Henkes
This story can help children to relate to "doing things their own way."

❏ *Seasons*
Author: Sarah Leslie
This book can help children to relate to weather and the activities they associate with each season.

❏ *The Snowy Day*
Author: Ezra Jack Keats
After reading this book, children can share their own snowy day experiences.

❏ *The Surprise Party*
Author: Annabelle Prager
This story can help children to recall a "surprise party" experience from their past.

❏ *There's a Monster Under My Bed*
Author: James Howe
Children can relate experiences of "being frightened by a monster in their bedroom."

❏ *Who's Going to Take Care of Me?*
Author: Michelle Magorian
After hearing this story, the children can use past experiences to define "how they are able to do something now that they could not do before."

Skill R 20: using mode or tone of voice

❏ *Effie*
Author: Beverly Allinson
Effie, a tiny ant, had a loud, booming voice. It was so loud that it scared away all the other insects. See if the students can change tone of voice as they read Effie's words which are printed in boldface type.

❏ *Hansel and Gretel: The Witch's Story*
Author: Sheila Black
This flip book tells the story from two points of view. Children can practice using tone of voice as the witch speaks.

Sight (cont.)

Skill R 20: using mode or tone of voice *(cont.)*

❑ *Jack and the Beanstalk*

Author: Steven Kellogg
While reading this book, the children can practice changing their tone of voice by trying to speak loudly and threateningly—as they believe that the giant might speak.

❑ *Goldilocks and the Three Bears*

Retold by: Armand Eisen
Children can practice changing their tone of voice by repeating the story phrases as they believe they would be said by Papa Bear, Mama Bear, and Baby Bear.

Skill R 21: using an example to define a word

❑ *Animal Homes*

Author: Sharon Elswit
This book provides information to define various types of animal homes.

❑ *Bears in the Night*

Authors: Stan and Jan Berenstain
After hearing this story, the students should be able to give definitions of concepts such as *on, through,* and *up.*

❑ *Happy Rhythms and Rhymes*

Poem: "Raindrop Small" (page 24)
Selected by: Patricia M. Cavanaugh
After reading this poem, children can give examples of "what rain can do."

❑ *Rhubarb*

Author: Stephen Cosgrove
After hearing this story, have children give examples of "qualities of friends."

❑ *The Wump World*

Author: Bill Peet
Children can give examples of "what might happen to our world if we do not become environmentally aware."

Skill R 22: recognizing and comparing irregular plural nouns to singular nouns

This objective can be met as the teacher encounters examples of irregular plural nouns that can be compared to singular nouns in oral reading to the class. No one book was found which contains many examples of this.

Auditory Perception

Skill R 23: listening to and reproducing sounds

❏ *The Berenstains' B Book*
Authors: Stan and Jan Berenstain
The sound associated with "B" is represented in nearly every word in this book. After the story, ask the children to name other words using "B" sounds.

❏ *Good-Night, Owl!*
Author: Pat Hutchins
Each page of this book reveals a forest animal and the sound that the animal makes. See if the students can reproduce these sounds.

❏ *Mister Brown Can Moo, Can You?*
Author: Dr. Seuss
Sounds that animals make are given here for students to reproduce.

❏ *My Barn*
Author: Craig Brown
This is a story telling all the animal sounds a boy loves to hear in his barn.

❏ *My First Easy and Fun Book All About Sounds*
Author: Ruth Thomson
A cow is asleep in the middle of the road. Jim, the children, and the animals try to make noises to awaken Daisy. Children can reproduce the sounds in the book.

❏ *Sound Words*
Author: Joan Hanson
This book gives words and illustrations that imitate sounds around us.

Skill R 24: listening to and identifying similar and different sounds

All the books listed below have a repetition of similar sounds and a variety of different sounds to examine.

❏ *A Dozen Dizzy Dogs*
Author: William H. Hooks

❏ *A Very Special House*
Author: Ruth Krauss

❏ *C Is for Clown*
Authors: Stan and Jan Berenstain

❏ *Eency Weency Spider*
Author: Joanne Oppenheim

❏ *The Cat in the Hat*
Author: Dr. Seuss

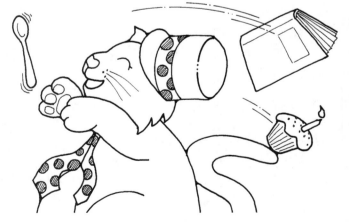

Skill R 25: identifying syllables heard in written and oral words

Any books having words with multiple syllables can be used to meet this objective.

Auditory Perception *(cont.)*

Skill R 26: matching consonant sounds

Each of the books and the poem listed below contain a variety of repeated consonant sounds for children to match.

❏ *Dr. Seuss's ABC*
Author: Dr. Seuss

❏ *C Is for Clown*
Author: Stan and Jan Berenstain

❏ *Crictor*
Author: Tomi Ungerer

❏ *Hound and Bear*
Author: Dick Gackenbach

❏ *A Snake Is Totally Tail*
Author: Judi Barrett

❏ *Something BIG Has Been Here*
Poem: "I Am Wunk" (page 20)
Author: Jack Prelutsky

❏ *Tikki Tikki Tembo*
Retold by: Arlene Mosel

Skill R 27: matching consonant blends and digraphs

The books and poems listed below contain many examples of words using consonant blends and digraphs.

❏ *A Beautiful Seashell*
Author: Ruth Lercher Bornstein

❏ *The Berenstain Bears' Christmas Tree*
Authors: Stan and Jan Berenstain

❏ *The Cat in the Hat Comes Back*
Author: Dr. Seuss

❏ *A New Treasury of Children's Poetry*
Poem: "Galoshes"
Selected by: Joanna Cole

❏ *Hand, Hand, Fingers, Thumb*
Author: Al Perkins

❏ *"I Can't" Said the Ant*
Author: Polly Cameron

❏ *Nathan and Nicholas Alexander*
Author: Lulu Delacre

Auditory Perception *(cont.)*

Skill R 28: matching vowels and vowel sounds

The books and poems listed below present many examples of vowels and vowel sounds for children to match.

❏ *Angus and the Cat*
Author: Marjorie Flack

❏ *Goodnight, Moon*
Author: Margaret Wise Brown

❏ *If You Give a Mouse a Cookie*
Author: Laura Joffe Numeroff

❏ *Something BIG Has Been Here*
Poem: "Kevin the King of the Jungle" (page 30)
Poem: "Watson Watts" (page 34)
Poem: "Life's Not Been the Same in My Family" (page 37)
Author: Jack Prelutsky

❏ *Puss in Boots*
Author: Charles Perrault

❏ *Swimmy*
Author: Leo Lionni

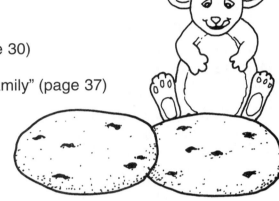

Word Analysis

Skill R 29: sounding out words beginning with consonant blends and digraphs

---

These books use many words beginning with consonant blends and diagraphs.

❏ *A Beautiful Seashell*
Author: Ruth Lercher Bornstein

❏ *The Cat in the Hat Comes Back*
Author: Dr. Seuss

❏ *Hand, Hand, Fingers, Thumb*
Author: Al Perkins

❏ *"I Can't" Said the Ant*
Author: Polly Cameron

❏ *Nathan and Nicholas Alexander*
Author: Lulu Delacre

Word Analysis

Skill R 30: sounding out one-syllable words with long vowel sounds

These books and poems present many one-syllable words with long vowel sounds.

- ❑ *A House Is a House for Me*
  Author: Many Ann Hoberman
- ❑ *An Anteater Named Arthur*
  Author: Bernard Weber
- ❑ *Happy Rhythms and Rhymes*
  Poem: "Autumn Leaf" (page 5)
  Selected by: Patricia M. Cavanaugh

- ❑ *Happy Rhythms and Rhymes*
  Poem: "Christmas Tree Angel"
  Selected by: Patricia M. Cavanaugh
- ❑ *The Mighty Hunter*
  Author: Berta and Elmer Hader
- ❑ *The Tooth Book*
  Author: Theo LeSieg

Skill R 31: sounding out one-syllable words with short vowel sounds

The books below use many one-syllable words with short vowel sounds.

- ❑ *A Tree Is Nice*
  Author: Janice May Udry
- ❑ *The Cat in the Hat*
  Author: Dr. Seuss
- ❑ *Clifford the Big Red Dog*
  Author: Norman Bridwell

- ❑ *Frog and Toad All Year*
  Author: Arnold Lobel
- ❑ *Great Day for Up*
  Author: Dr. Seuss
- ❑ *The Story of Johnny Appleseed*
  Author: Aliki

Skill R 32: sounding out one-syllable words with vowel combinations

One-syllable words with vowel combinations are frequently repeated in the following books.

- ❑ *Circus*
  Author: Lois Ehlert
- ❑ *Green Eggs and Ham*
  Author: Dr. Seuss
- ❑ *Something BIG Has Been Here*
  Poem: "I Met a Rat of Culture" (page 38)
  Author: Jack Prelutsky
- ❑ *Something BIG Has Been Here*
  Poem: "Kevin the King of the Jungle" (page 30)
  Author: Jack Prelutsky

- ❑ *Poems Children Will Sit Still For*
  Poem: "Rain Poem" (page 24)
  Compiled by: The editors of Scholastic's Lucky Book Club
- ❑ *Seeds and More Seeds*
  Author: Millicent E. Selsam
- ❑ *Something BIG Has Been Here*
  Poem: "We're Four Ferocious Tigers" (page 11)
  Author: Jack Prelutsky

Word Analysis *(cont.)*

Skill R 33: sounding out one-syllable words with digraphs

These books and poems frequently use one-syllable words with digraphs.

❑ *Something BIG Has Been Here*
Poem: "I Wave Goodbye When Butter Flies" (page 80)
Poem: "The Barber of Shrubbery Hollow" (page 128)
Poem: "Wilhelmina Wafflewitz" (page 83)
Author: Jack Prelutsky

❑ *Sheep in a Jeep*
Author: Nancy Shaw

❑ *Sheep in a Shop*
Author: Nancy Shaw

Skill R 34: building and using new words using the same ending

The books listed below represent examples for use in building new words using the same endings.

❑ *Andy: That's My Name*
Author: Tomie dePaola

❑ *Hop on Pop*
Author: Dr. Seuss

❑ *A New Treasury of Children's Poetry*
Poem: "Little Black Bug" (page 23)
Selected by: Joanna Cole

❑ *There's a Wocket in My Pocket*
Author: Dr. Seuss

❑ *There's an Ant in Anthony*
Author: Bernard Most

❑ *Something BIG Has Been Here*
Poem: "Twaddletalk Tuck" (page 64)
Author: Jack Prelutsky

❑ *Poems Children Will Sit Still For*
Poem: "Weather"
Compiled by: Editors of Scholastic's Lucky Book Club

❑ *Zug the Bug*
Author: Colin and Jacqui Hawkins

Structural Analysis

Skill R 35: reading words with same ending sounds

The above books or any other books which repeat sounds that need to be stressed could be used to meet these objectives.

Skill R 36: identifying prefix, suffix, and root words in affixed words

The books listed below give several examples of affixed words.

❏ *A Wall of Names*
   Author: Judy Donnelly
❏ *Frog and Toad Are Friends*
   Author: Arnold Lobel
❏ *How My Garden Grew*
   Author: Anne and Harlow Rockwell
❏ *Proud Pumpkin*
   Author: Nora S. Unwin
❏ *Sam the Minuteman*
   Author: Nathaniel Benchley
❏ *Good Books, Good Times*
   Poem: "What If?" (page 21)
   Selected by: Lee Bennett Hopkins

Skill R 37: reading and building compound words

The books listed below give examples of compound words within the text of the stories.

❏ *Backyard Basketball Superstar*
   Author: Monica Klein
❏ *Cloudy with a Chance of Meatballs*
   Author: Judi Barrett
❏ *In a People House*
   Author: Theo LeSieg
❏ *The Lost Present*
   Author: Angela Holroyd
❏ *Remember the Butterflies*
   Author: Anna Grossnickle Hines

Structural Analysis *(cont.)*

Skill R 38: Reading and building contractions—apostrophe usage

- ❑ *Something BIG Has Been Here*
  Poem: "An Elephant Is Hard to Hide" (page 148)
  Poem: "Mosquitoes, Mosquitoes!" (page 136)
  Author: Jack Prelutsky
- ❑ *The Berenstain Bears Don't Pollute (Anymore)*
  Authors: Stan and Jan Berenstain
- ❑ *Pet Show!*
  Author: Ezra Jack Keats
- ❑ *Peter's Chair*
  Author: Ezra Jack Keats

Skill R 39: reading possessives—singular, plural, and apostrophe usage

The books and the poems listed below give examples of possessives.
- ❑ *Bear's Magic and Other Stories*
  Author: Carla Stevens
- ❑ *Clifford's Word Book*
  Author: Norman Bridwell
- ❑ *Many Luscious Lollipops*
  Author: Ruth Heller
- ❑ *Merry-Go-Round*
  Author: Ruth Heller
- ❑ *Something BIG Has Been Here*
  Poem: "My Brother's Bug" (page 151)
  Author: Jack Prelutsky
- ❑ *Peter's Chair*
  Author: Ezra Jack Keats

Literal

Skill R 40: following stated directions

❑ *The Berenstain Bears Learn About Strangers*
Authors: Jan and Stan Berenstain
A list of rules for children to follow regarding strangers is given on the last page. Situations can be role-played.

❑ *I Did It . . .*
Author: Harlow Rockwell
Six simple art projects are explained step by step in this book.

❑ *The Little Pigs Puppet Book*
Author: N. Cameron Watson
Directions are stated along with illustrations to make three types of puppets.

❑ *The Secret Birthday Message*
Author: Eric Carle
Tim finds a secret message describing directions for him to follow to reach a birthday surprise. Students can follow the directions along with him.

❑ *Valentine Friends*
Author: Ann Schweninger
Written directions along with illustrations are given to make valentines.

Skill R 41: recalling stated details

❑ *Chickens Aren't the Only Ones*
Author: Ruth Heller
Children can recall details about eggs and the animals that lay them.

❑ *Humphrey—The Lost Whale*
Authors: Wendy Tokuda and Richard Hall
Humphrey the whale left the ocean and entered the San Francisco Bay and then the Sacramento River. This is a true story about how the people of San Francisco helped to get Humphrey back out to sea. After reading the story, see how many details of Humphrey's escape the students can remember.

❑ *The Panda*
Author: Yvette Metral
This book is divided into parts separated by boldface subtitles which explain an aspect of the panda's life. After the story, children can recall "panda facts."

❑ *The Wind Thief*
Author: Judi Barrett
Have children recall "real" and "make-believe" characteristics of the wind.

❑ *What Makes It Rain? The Story of a Raindrop*
Author: Keith Brandt
Much information about rain and rainfall is given in this book. After reading the story, students can recall some of these "rain facts."

Literal (cont.)

Skills R 42: identifying stated causes and effects in written material

---

❏ *The Big Sneeze*

Author: Ruth Brown

A sneeze by the farmer causes a whole series of events to take place in the barn.

❏ *The House That Had Enough*

Author: P. E. King

Anne had not taken care of her bed, clothing, toys, etc., so these items all decide to leave for a home where someone will take care of them.

❏ *If You Give a Mouse a Cookie*

Author: Laura Joffe Numeroff

Each time the mouse is given something, it causes him to want something else.

❏ *Jim and the Beanstalk*

Author: Raymond Briggs

Each time the giant decides to eat Jim, a way for Jim to help the giant is discovered instead. Jim helps the giant, and soon they become friends.

❏ *The Napping House*

Author: Audrey Wood

This is a humorous, sequential tale where the bite from a flea causes a whole series of events to happen to all of the creatures in the Napping House.

❏ *The Runaway Bunny*

Author: Margaret Wise Brown

This story shows the love of a mother rabbit for her son. He wants to run away, but each place that he decides to go, mother has a reason to go there, too.

Inferential

Skill R 43: drawing conclusions implied in reading passages

❏ *Annie and the Wild Animals*

Author: Jan Brett

Annie's cat, Taffy, is missing one winter morning when Annie goes to look for her. Annie desires a new animal friend, so she places corn cakes at the edge of the woods to see which animal comes to eat. She finds a different animal each morning eating the corn cakes. The text gives a reason for each wild animal being unsuitable for a pet.

Children can draw conclusions as to which animals would be good pets and why. Also, the border illustrations help the reader draw conclusions about what happens to Taffy.

Inferential (cont.)

Skill R 43: drawing conclusions implied in reading passages (cont.)

❑ *Cloudy with a Chance of Meatballs*
Author: Judi Barrett
Children can draw conclusions as to what will happen to the town of Chewandswallow after all the townspeople leave. Various other opportunities for drawing conclusions are provided within this story.

❑ *Grandpa and Bo*
Author: Kevin Henkes
At the end of the book, Grandpa and Bo make the same wish. The wish is never stated, but the reader is led to the wish by clues given throughout the story.

❑ *Guess What?*
Author: Roger Bester
Pictures with matching text clues are given to help children draw conclusions as to what item is being described.

❑ *What Am I?*
Author: Stephanie Calmenson
Each page tells a rhyming riddle about a mystery item. The students draw conclusions as to the identity. The mystery is solved by turning the page.

Skill R 44: comparing and contrasting ideas in reading selections

❑ *Is It Larger? Is It Smaller?*
Author: Tana Hoban
This wordless book use photographs of objects to compare and contrast.

❑ *Is It Rough? Is It Smooth? Is It Shiny?*
Author: Tana Hoban
Photographs of common items or scenes are presented for students to visually compare and contrast textures.

❑ *Jack and the Beanstalk*
Author: Steven Kellogg

❑ *Jim and the Beanstalk*
Author: Raymond Briggs
Compare and contrast these two tales.

❑ *The Little House*
Author: Virginia Lee Burton
This book compares and contrasts city and country living.

❑ *The Perfect Spot*
Author: Robert J. Blake
A father and son go into the woods looking for "the perfect spot." Each place is rejected because the setting is not perfect for Dad's painting. Have children compare and contrast all of the "spots," including "the perfect spot."

Inferential (cont.)

Skill 44: comparing and contrasting ideas in reading selections (cont.)

❏ *What's Alike? What's Different?*
Authors: Selma and Jack Wasserman
This book shows many ways to compare items. A bicycle and a wagon are compared by examining the number of wheels, how they move, what they look like, and what each can carry.

❏ *When I Was Young in the Mountains*
Author: Cynthia Rylant
Children can compare and contrast events described in this story with the way that they do those same things in their own lives today.

❏ *When the Rain Stops*
Author: Sheila Cole
This book compares the woods before and after a summer rain.

Skill R 45: stating a simplified analysis of a character in a story

Each of the stories below presents strong examples of characterization.
Characters with traits opposite those of the main characters are also presented.

❏ *Alexander and the Wind-up Mouse*
Author: Leo Lionni

❏ *Angry Arthur*
Author: Hiawyn Oram

❏ *Chrysanthemum*
Author: Kevin Henkes

❏ *Miss Nelson Is Missing*
Author: Harry Allard

❏ *Peter Rabbit*
Author: Beatrix Potter

Skill R 46: demonstrating empathy with characters in a story

The books listed below contain characters who express strong emotions. See if students can relate how the characters feel in given situations.

❏ *Best Friends*
Author: Steven Kellogg

❏ *Corduroy*
Author: Don Freeman

❏ *Hey Al*
Author: Arthur Yorinks

❏ *Little Wolf and the Giant*
Author: Sue Porter

❏ *Mama One, Mama Two*
Author: Patricia MacLachlan

Skill R 47: summarizing a written passage

❏ *A Hippopotamus Ate the Teacher*
Author: Mike Thaler
The children will have fun summarizing this simple story plot about a hippopotamus that ate a teacher.

Inferential (cont.)

Skill R 47: summarizing a written passage *(cont.)*

❑ *Just a Dream*
   Author: Chris Van Allsburg
   A boy becomes environmentally conscious because of a dream about the world in the future. Children can summarize the story by giving examples of the boy's actions before, during, and after the dream.

❑ *The Little Girl and the Big Bear*
   Author: Joanna Galdone
   This simple story plot would be good for beginning summarizing. A little girl is captured by a bear and made to be a servant. Near the end of the story, the girl tricks the bear into taking her home.

❑ *Once Upon MacDonald's Farm*
   Author: Stephen Gammell
   Since this version is so different from the traditional version, children will note the silly differences presented in this book. The plot is simple yet original. This will lend itself well to beginning summarizing.

❑ *Stone Soup*
   Author: Marilyn Sapienza
   This simple plot about sharing is easy to summarize.

Skill R 48: stating the main idea in a written passage

❑ *Barn Dance!*
   Authors: Bill Martin, Jr. and John Archambault
   See if children can state this main idea of a boy and the barn animals having a wonderful time dancing in the barn by moonlight.

❑ *The Big Snow*
   Authors: Berta and Elmer Hader
   This book presents many woodland animals along with information about what each animal does to prepare for winter and how food is obtained by the animals during the big snow. See if children can state this main idea.

❑ *Flip*
   Author: Wesley Dennis
   The life of a young colt is observed in this book along with some of his thoughts and feelings. The students should be able to tell this main idea after hearing the story.

❑ *The Reason for a Flower*
   Author: Ruth Heller
   The main idea of seeds being the reason for a flower is clearly stated within this book. Children can pick up more information about plants and seeds by studying the detailed illustrations.

Application

Skill R 49: applying previously learned information to a new situation

❑ *Color Farm*

Author: Lois Ehlert

Children view shapes in a new way and are encouraged to use common shapes to create animals.

❑ *Each Orange Has 8 Slices: A Counting Book*

Author: Paul Giganti, Jr.

This book takes common objects and turns them into counting experiences. Example: I saw two cows, each had four legs. How many legs are there?

❑ *A New Treasury of Children's Poetry*

Poem: "Houses" (page 185)
Selected by: Joanna Cole

Houses are described as faces, with the text and illustrations working together to portray this new way of looking at houses.

❑ *Molly's Pilgrim*

Author: Barbara Cohen

The definition of pilgrim is given through an example with which children can relate. This will broaden their personal definitions of *pilgrim*.

❑ *Paper, Paper Everywhere*

Author: Gail Gibbons

Children are familiar with what paper is and some of its uses, but now they can see where paper comes from and how it gets from tree to paper.

❑ *Q Is for Duck*

Authors: Mary Elting and Michael Folsom

This book does not approach the alphabet in a traditional way. The initial letter used is not from the subject being focused upon; instead, the initial letter is from a characteristic related to that subject. For example: B is for dog. Why? Because a dog barks.

Critical

Skill R 50: distinguishing facts from opinions in a story

❑ *A Flea Story*

Author: Leo Lionni

Two fleas on a dog express different opinions about leaving the dog to explore the world.

❑ *The Great Kapok Tree*

Author: Lynne Cherry

Several rain forest animals whisper their opinions in the man's ear as to why the great kapok tree should not be cut down.

❑ *Hidden Treasure*

Auther: Pamela Allen

After hearing this story, students can express their opinions as to which brother was better off over the years.

❑ *How to Train Your Puppy*

Author: Kurt Unkelbach

Several facts and opinions about training a puppy are expressed in this book.

❑ *Old MacDonald Had an Apartment House*

Author: Judith Barret

Old MacDonald is the manager of an apartment building. Tenants keep moving out because of problems created from MacDonald planting fruits and vegetables in unoccupied rooms. MacDonald claims that fruits and vegetables make better tenants than people. Children can state whether they agree with this opinion or not.

Oral Reading Skills

Skill R 51: orally reading and interpreting sentences, using punctuation and phrasing

❑ *Chicka Chicka Boom Boom*
Authors: Bill Martin, Jr. and John Archambault
This delightful rhythmic story lends itself well to reading in phrases.

❑ *Hide and Snake*
Author: Keith Baker
The rhythm of this book lends itself to reading the phrasing which mixes the use of commas and periods.

❑ *A New Treasury of Children's Poetry*
Poem: "Hug O'War" (page 60)
Selected by: Joanna Cole
Rhythm and rhyme makes this poem easy to read in phrases.

❑ *I Know an Old Lady Who Swallowed a Fly*
Retold by: Nadine Bernard Westcott
The phrases in this book are very important to the meaning of the tale.

❑ *Mrs. Huggins and Her Hen Hannah*
Author: Lydia Dabcovich
This book uses short related phrases to coincide with the illustrations.

❑ *Poems Children Will Sit Still For*
Poem: "Our Tree" (page 18)
Compiled by: Editors of Scholastic's Lucky Book Club
An apple tree in each of the four seasons is described in this poem which uses commas and periods to separate phrases and sentences.

❑ *Wild Horses of the Red Desert*
Author: Glen Rounds
Many sentences using commas are presented in this book.

Silent Reading Skills

Skill R 52: demonstrating comprehension of material read silently

Any book that a child has read can be used to meet this objective if the child is able to discuss the main elements of plot, setting, and characterization..

Literal Understanding

Skill R 53: identifying the stated main idea heard in a story

❑ *Animals Should Definitely Not Wear Clothing* and *Animals Should Definitely Not Act Like People*

Author: Judi Barrett
In the above books by Judi Barrett, put construction paper over the covers so that the children can't see them. Read the stories. Ask students to tell what the whole story was about.

❑ *The Berenstain Bears and the Prize Pumpkin*

Authors: Stan and Jan Berenstain
Father Bear's mind is taken off the true meaning of Thanksgiving in an effort to beat Farmer Ben at growing the largest pumpkin. By the end of the story, the Bears' minds are back on being thankful at Thanksgiving. See if the students can pick up on this main idea.

❑ *Good Books, Good Times*

Selected by: Lee Bennett Hopkins
Read the collection of poems in this book to students. Ask the students to name what all of the poems are about. See if the main idea—fun with books—is discovered.

❑ *Plants That Never Ever Bloom*

Author: Ruth Heller
Conceal the covers of the book so that the children cannot see the title or the cover illustrations. Read the story, sharing the illustrations. When the reading is completed, ask what the book was about. This should produce the main idea.

❑ *Trees*

Author: Ruth Thomson
Cover the bold-faced headings on each page. Read the information one page at a time. Ask students to tell what all the information on the page is about. This should produce the main idea for each page.

Skills R 54: recalling stated sequential events heard in a story

❑ *A House for Hermit Crab*

Author: Eric Carle
Hermit visits many sea creatures, inviting them to live on or near his shell. The sequence of these visiting creatures may be recalled.

❑ *At Mary Bloom's*

Author: Aliki
Mary Bloom's friend tells a sequence of events that she believes will happen if she takes her new baby mice to Mary's house.

❑ *The Biggest Little House in the Forest*

Author: Djemma Bider
One at a time animals come to live in the little house in the woods. Each time a new animal comes, the previous residents are introduced.

Literal Understanding (cont.)

Skill R 54: recalling stated sequential events heard in a story (cont.)

❑ *Deep Down Underground*
Author: Olivier Dunrea
Each line is repeated in order as all of the underground animals hear the moudiewort digging.

❑ *The House on Maple Street*
Author: Bonnie Pryor
A family's property is viewed in the sequence that it developed over the years since the first settlers.

❑ *The Mitten*
Author: Jan Brett
One by one animals come out of the forest to find warmth in Nikki's mitten. The next repeats the previous visitors each time a new visitor comes to the mitten.

❑ *The Napping House*
Author: Audrey Wood
A young boy and some animals crawl on top of granny to sleep. As each one comes, the others are repeated.

❑ *The Ox-Cart Man*
Author: Donald Hall
This story is about a family using natural resources and nature to make items to sell at the market. The end of the story gives clues to the sequence beginning all over again.

❑ *Pancakes, Pancakes*
Author: Eric Carle
Jack wants pancakes for breakfast. For each ingredient needed, Jack has to go right to the source. Children can be asked to recall the ingredients needed to make the pancakes or the steps Jack went through to get the ingredients.

❑ *This Is the House That Jack Built*
Author: Liz Underhill
Each page introduces a new item or creature that acts upon the previously mentioned item. All of the items are stated each time.

❑ *The Turnip*
Retold by: Janina Domanska
Grandma, grandpa, and several animals come one at a time to help pull the enormous turnip from the ground. Each person or creature comes to pull on the one in front.

❑ *The Very Hungry Caterpillar*
Author: Eric Carle
In sequence with the days of the week, a hungry caterpillar eats through a variety of foods until on the last day he eats too much—which results in a stomach ache.

Critical Listening

Skill R 55: selecting critical details heard in a story

❏ *A Little Excitement*
Author: Marc Harshman
This delightful story tells about a family living in the country in the winter. Willie is bored and wishes for some excitement. The "excitement" comes in the form of danger which ends up drawing the family closer. Children can identify details about fire safety.

❏ *The Mixed-Up Chameleon*
Author: Eric Carle
Ask children to tell why the chameleon decides that he does not want to be any of the other animals that he previously wished to be.

❏ *Strangers*
Author: Dorothy Chlad
Children will select critical details about strangers and tell how they can apply what they heard to their own lives.

Fiction

Skill R 56: listening to and reading fiction stories

Provide children with a variety of fiction books to meet this objective.

Nonfiction

Skill R 57: listening to and reading nonfiction stories

Provide children with a variety of nonfiction books to meet this objective.

Poetry

Skill R 58: listening to and reading poetry

Provide children with a variety of poetry selections to meet this objective.

Parts of Speech

Skill L 1: recognizing singular and plural nouns

The books listed below give examples of singular and plural nouns.
- ❑ *Anatole*
  Author: Eve Titus
- ❑ *Happy Rhythms and Rhymes*
  Poem: "Bees" (page 15)
  Author: Patricia M. Cavanaugh
- ❑ *The Icky Bug Book*
  Author: Jerry Pallotta
- ❑ *Merry-Go-Round*
  Author: Ruth Heller
- ❑ *The Yucky Reptile Book*
  Author: Jerry Pallotta

Skill L 2: recognizing regular verbs in the present, past, and future tenses

These books give examples of verbs in either past tense, present tense, future tense, or a combination of tenses.
- ❑ *Kites Sail High*
  Author: Ruth Heller
- ❑ *Sarah, Plain and Tall*
  Author: Patricia MacLachlan
- ❑ *What Happened to Patrick's Dinosaurs?*
  Author: Carol Carrick

Skill L 3: recognizing and using subject-verb agreement

This objective may be taught from any book in which examples of sentences using subject-verb agreement are present.

Skill L 4: recognizing singular and plural personal pronouns

These poems give examples of singular and plural personal pronouns for students to locate.
- ❑ *A New Treasury of Children's Poetry*
  Poem: "Bats" (page 97)
  Poem: "Little" (page 52)
  Poem: "The Little Turtle" (page 22)
  Selected by: Joanna Cole

Parts of Speech *(cont.)*

Skill L 4: recognizing singular and plural personal pronouns *(cont.)*

❑ *A New Treasury of Children's Poetry*
Poem: "The Owl and the Pussycat" (page 104)
Poem: "Tree Toad" (page 97)
Selected by: Joanna Cole

❑ *Where the Sidewalk Ends*
Poem: "Us" (page 36)
Author: Shel Silverstein

Skill L 5: recognizing polite pronoun order

As examples of polite pronoun order are encountered in reading with children, the sentences can be pulled from the text to examine more closely.

Skill L 6: recognizing double negatives

The poems listed below give examples of double negatives. Use these examples to demonstrate to children why not to use double negatives.

❑ *A New Treasury of Children's Poetry*
Poem: "The Frog" (page 96)
Selected by: Joanna Cole

Poem: "Mother to Son" (page 50)
Poem: "Mr. 'Gator" (page 93)
Selected by: Joanna Cole

❑ *Where the Sidewalk Ends*
Poem: "The Unicorn" (pages 76 and 77)
Author: Shel Silverstein

❑ *More Poetry for Holidays*
Poem: "Valentine" (page 11)
Selected by: Nancy Larrick

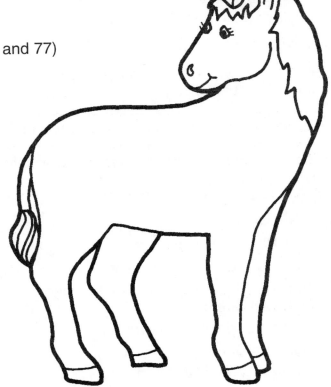

Capitalization

Skill L 7: capitalizing the first word of a sentence

Capitalizing the first word of a sentence can be taught using any book.

Skill L 8: capitalizing proper nouns

The books listed below give examples of capitalization of proper nouns.

❏ *Arthur's Thanksgiving*
Author: Marc Brown

❏ *Best Thanksgiving Book: ABC Adventures*
Author: Pat Whitehead

❏ *The Biggest Little House in the Forest*
Author: Djemma Bider

❏ *Clifford's Family*
Author: Norman Bridwell

❏ *George and Matilda Mouse and the Floating School*
Author: Heather S. Buchanan

❏ *Grandpa and Bo*
Author: Kevin Henkes

❏ *Hooper Humperdink . . . ? Not Him*
Author: Theo LeSieg

❏ *Oh, What a Thanksgiving!*
Author: Steven Kroll

❏ *Stars*
Author: Seymour Simon

❏ *The Surprise Party*
Author: Annabelle Prager

Skill L 9: capitalizing days of the week and months of the year

These books show days and months correctly capitalized.

❏ *The First of October*
Author: Theo LeSieg

❏ *Our House on the Hill*
Author: Philippe Dupasquier

❏ *Something BIG Has Been Here*
Poem: "The Rain in Little Dribbles" (page 53)
Author: Jack Prelutsky

❏ *The Very Hungry Caterpillar*
Author: Eric Carle

❏ *The Year at Maple Hill Farm*
Authors: Alice and Martin Provensen

Capitalization *(cont.)*

Skill L 10: capitalizing holidays

The books below use names of holidays correctly capitalized.

❑ *Arthur's Thanksgiving*
   Author: Marc Brown
❑ *It's Valentine's Day*
   Author: Jack Prelutsky
❑ *Oh, What a Thanksgiving!*
   Author: Steven Kroll
❑ *Over and Over*
   Author: Charlotte Zolotow
❑ *The Twelve Days of Christmas*
   Author: Jan Brett

Skill L 11: capitalizing the personal pronoun *I*

These books frequently use the pronoun *I* in varying positions within sentences.

❑ *Happy Birthday, Moon*
   Author: Frank Asch
❑ *Happy Birthday to Me*
   Authors: Anne and Harlow Rockwell
❑ *I'm Alvin*
   Author: Elizabeth Rice

❑ *Snow Company*
   Author: Marc Harshman
❑ *Sometimes I'm Afraid*
   Author: Sylvia Root Tester

Skill L 12: capitalizing titles before proper names

The following books give representations of capitalized titles before proper names.

❑ *The Day It Rained Watermelons*
   Author: Mable Watts
❑ *Mr. Rabbit and the Lovely Present*
   Author: Charlotte Zolotow

❑ *Mrs. Huggins and Her Hen Hannah*
   Author: Lydia Dabcovich

Skill L 13: capitalizing initials of persons' names

❑ *Mystery of the Runaway Sled*
   Author: Erica Frost

Skill L 14: capitalizing parts of addresses

❑ *Kate Heads West*
   Author: Pat Brisson

Punctuation

Skill L 15: using periods after declarative and imperative sentences

Any book using periods at the ends of declarative or imperative sentences can be used to meet this objective.

Skill L 16: using periods after numbers, initials, and abbreviations

Books containing many examples of abbreviations were not found. However, these can be pointed out as they naturally appear in any written text.

Skill L 17: using commas to separate items in addresses

❑ *Kate Heads West*
Author: Pat Brisson
This objective can be met by modeling how to properly address envelopes. The students can then practice addressing envelopes to book characters.

Skill L 18: using commas to separate items when writing the date

The books listed below present examples of using a comma to separate items when writing the date.

❑ *Dear Annie*
Author: Judith Casely

❑ *Kate Heads West*
Author: Pat Brisson

❑ *Sarah, Plain and Tall*
Author: Patricia MacLachlan

❑ *Your Best Friend, Kate*
Author: Pat Brisson

Skill L 19: using commas after the greeting and closing in personal letters

These books show personal letters in which commas have been used after the greeting and closing.

❑ *Dear Annie*
Author: Judith Caseley

❑ *Kate Heads West*
Author: Pat Brisson

❑ *Sarah, Plain and Tall*
Author: Patricia MacLachlan

❑ *Your Best Friend, Kate*
Author: Pat Brisson

Punctuation *(cont.)*

Skill L 20: using a question mark after an interrogative sentence

The following books repeatedly give examples of using question marks after interrogative sentences.

❏ *Are You My Mother?*

Author: P. D. Eastman
A baby bird is hatched alone. She wanders from animal to object, asking "Are you my mother?"

❏ *The Biggest, Smallest, Fastest, Tallest Things You've Ever Heard Of*

Author: Robert Lopshire
Each page asks a question about something that is the biggest, smallest, fastest, or tallest in the world.

❏ *Even If I Did Something Awful*

Author: Barbara Shook Hazen
A young girl continuously asks her mother questions pertaining to the amount of love her mother has for her.

❏ *Is Your Mama a Llama?*

Author: Deborah Guarino
A young llama asks other animal babies if their mamas are llamas. Each answers, giving a distinctive feature which makes it different from a llama.

❏ *The Manners Book*

Author: June Behrens
A little boy encounters situations where manners or formal language is appropriate. He asks his teddy bear, Ned, what to do in each situation.

❏ *Maybe You Should Fly a Jet! Maybe You Should Be a Vet!*

Author: Theodore Le Sieg
Questions pertaining to careers are given in this book.

❏ *Mr. Rabbit and the Lovely Present*

Author: Charlotte Zolotow
While trying to help a young girl find the perfect gift for her mother, Mr. Rabbit asks questions to find out what the girl's mother likes and dislikes.

Punctuation *(cont.)*

Skill L 20: using a question mark after an interrogative sentence *(cont.)*

❑ *What Is Beyond the Hill?*
Author: Ernst A. Ekker

❑ *A New Treasury of Children's Poetry*
Poem: "Where Have You Been, Dear?" (page 201)
Selected by: Joanna Cole

❑ *Would You Rather Be a Bullfrog?*
Author: Theo Le Sieg
This book asks questions about what the reader would rather be.

Skill L 21: using an exclamation point at the end of an exclamatory sentence

---

The books and poems listed below give examples of the use of an exclamation point at the end of an exclamatory sentence.

❑ *Something BIG Has Been Here*
Poem: "Belinda Blue" (page 16)
Poem: "Hello! How Are You? I Am Fine!" (page 36)
Poem: "The Zoo Was in an Uproar" (page 62)
Author: Jack Prelutsky

❑ *The Snow Child*
Retold by: Freya Littledale

❑ *Sylvester and the Magic Pebble*
Author: William Steig

Sentences

Skill L 22: writing a sentence using a simple subject and verb

---

Any book using examples of sentences with simple subjects and verbs can be used to teach this objective.

Skill L 23: writing a sentence with agreement of subject and verb

---

Any book using examples of sentences with subject-verb agreement can be used to teach this objective.

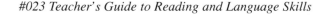

Paragraph

Skill L 24: identifying the topic sentence of a paragraph

The following books lend themselves to the identification of a topic sentence in a paragraph.

- ❑ *A Picture Book of Benjamin Franklin*
  Author: David A. Adler
- ❑ *Ladybird First Facts About Animals*
  Author: Caroline Arnold
- ❑ *I Can Read About Whales and Dolphins*
  Author: J.I. Anderson

- ❑ *Let's Visit a Chocolate Factory*
  Author: Catherine O'Neill
- ❑ *Let's Visit a Toy Factory*
  Author: Miriam Anne Bourne
- ❑ *The Turtle*
  Author: Yvette Metral

Composition Objectives

Skill L 25: writing a short creative composition

- ❑ *Alphabet Soup*
  Author: Kate Banks
  While eating alphabet soup, a boy and a bear go on an imaginary trip facing many dilemmas. Each dilemma is solved by the boy putting his spoon into his soup to spell a word needed to solve the problem. Students can use this theme as a model for their own creative compositions.

- ❑ *The Birthday Moon*
  Author: Lois Duncan
  A fairy gives a little girl the moon for her birthday. Each phase of the moon (whole, half, quarter) becomes an everyday, useful item as the fairy explains how each phase can be used. Children can use this story as a model for writing a composition about using an object from nature in many useful, creative ways.

- ❑ *Clifford's Pals*
  Author: Norman Bridwell
  Because Clifford is so big, he gets into lots of trouble. Have students write stories about a huge dog that gets into trouble because of his size.

- ❑ *I Had a Little . . .*
  Author: Norma Levarie
  After hearing this book read aloud, children can use the same pattern to create cumulative, rhyming phrases of their own.

- ❑ *The Long, Green Pencil*
  Author: Sara Werner
  Lizzie finds a long, green pencil. She discovers that whatever she writes about with that pencil comes true.
  Children can write their own stories that they wish would come true.

Composition Objectives *(cont.)*

Skill L 25: writing a short creative composition *(cont.)*

❏ *Miss Rumphius*
Author: Barbara Cooney
Alice had wanted three things in her lifetime: to live by the sea, to travel to far away places, and to make the world more beautiful. Have children write a composition stating where they would most like to live, a place they would most like to visit, and a way that they could make the world more beautiful.

Skill L 26: writing poetry

Present children with many examples and styles of poetry before they begin to write their own. Here are some specific and general sources that can be used to meet this objective.

❏ *A New Treasury of Children's Poetry*
Poem: "Eletelephony" (page 102)
Selected by: Joanna Cole

❏ *Hawk, I'm Your Brother*
Author: Byrd Baylor

❏ *Something BIG Has Been Here*
Poem: "I Should Have Stayed in Bed Today" (page 28)
Author: Jack Prelutsky

❏ *When Clay Sings*
Author: Byrd Baylor

❏ *Where the Sidewalk Ends*
Author: Shel Silverstein

Letter Objectives

Skill L 27: identifying heading, greeting, body, closing, and signature of a letter; arranging a letter neatly

❏ *Kate Heads West*
Author: Pat Brisson

Skill 28: identifying the return address on an envelope; writing a block-style address on an envelope

Books giving accurate examples of these objectives were not to be found. This objective can be met using teacher modeling and address information about book characters.

Major Literary Convention Objectives

Skill L 29: recognizing and using wordless picture books

All of the following books contain illustrations only. The illustrations are arranged in such a way that students can infer the storyline from one illustration to the next to make a meaningful story.

❑ *A Boy, a Dog, a Frog and a Friend*
Authors: Mercer and Marianna Mayer

❑ *Carl's Afternoon in the Park*
Author: Alexandra Day

❑ *Do You Want to Be My Friend?*
Author: Eric Carle

❑ *Free Fall*
Author: David Wiesner

❑ *Frog Goes to Dinner*
Author: Mercer Mayer

❑ *Frog on His Own*
Author: Mercer Mayer

❑ *Frog, Where Are You?*
Author: Mercer Mayer

❑ *Good Dog, Carl*
Author: Alexandra Day

❑ *The Hunter and the Animals*
Author: Tomie dePaola

❑ *Junglewalk*
Author: Nancy Tafuri

❑ *Just in Passing*
Author: Susan Bonners

❑ *Noah's Ark*
Author: Peter Spier

❑ *One Frog Too Many*
Author: Mercer and Marianna Mayer

❑ *Rain*
Author: Peter Spier

❑ *Window*
Author: Jeannie Baker

Major Literary Convention Objectives (cont.)

Skill L 30: recognizing and using creative dramatics

These books contain plots which would be easy to dramatize.

❏ *Caps for Sale*
Author: Esphyr Slobodkina

❏ *Crictor*
Author: Tomi Ungerer

❏ *Eency Weency Spider*
Author: Joanne Oppenheim

❏ *Gregory, the Terrible Eater*
Author: Mitchell Sharmat

❏ *Ira Sleeps Over*
Author: Bernard Waber

❏ *The Runaway Bunny*
Author: Margaret Wise Brown

Skill L 31: recognizing and using nursery rhymes

❏ *Father Gander Nursery Rhymes: The Equal Rhymes Amendment*
Author: Dr. Douglas W. Larche
The author adds verses to the traditional "Mother Goose Nursery Rhymes." If a "Mother Goose" rhyme has a female main character, the author adds a new verse with a male main character (and vice versa).

❏ *Four and Twenty Dinosaurs*
Author: Bernard Most
Dinosaurs are the subject of this nursery rhyme book. Traditional nursery rhymes are used with the substitution of a dinosaur either within the text or within the illustrations.

❏ *In a Pumpkin Shell*
Author: Joan Walsh Anglund
The author arranges this alphabet book by reciting nursery rhymes relating to each letter of the alphabet.

❏ *The Real Mother Goose*
Selected by: Blanche Fisher Wright
Traditional and untraditional nursery rhymes are presented in this book.

Skill L 32: recognizing song

❏ *Eency Weency Spider*
Author: Joanne Oppenheim

❏ *Over in the Meadow*
Author: Paul Galdone

❏ *Over the River and Through the Woods*
Author: Normand Chartier

❏ *The Twelve Days of Christmas*
Author: Jan Brett

❏ *The Wheels on the Bus*
Author: Maryann Kovalski

Major Literary Convention Objectives (cont.)

Skill L 33: recognizing rhyming endings in poetry

Any poem with rhyming endings can be used to meet this objective. Here is a list of some children's favorites.

❑ *Happy Rhythms and Rhymes*
Poem: "Christmas Lights" (page 10)
Poem: "The Snowman and the Bunny" (page 11)
Selected by: Patricia M. Cavanaugh

❑ *A New Treasury of Children's Poetry*
Poem: "Holding Hands" (page 81)
Selected by: Joanna Cole

❑ *Something BIG Has Been Here*
Poem: "My Brother's Bug" (page 151)
Poem: "The Turkey Shot Out of the Oven" (page 18)
Poem: "Twaddletalk Tuck" (page 64)
Author: Jack Prelutsky

❑ *My Shadow*
Author: Robert Louis Stevenson

Levels

Skill L 34: distinguishing between casual and attentive listening

After each title, the word "casual" or "attentive" is listed to tell the level of listening that the child needs to be engaged in while listening to the stories.

❏ *Good Work, Amelia Bedelia*
   Author: Peggy Parish
   (casual listening)

❏ *The House That Jack Built*
   Author: Randolph Caldecott
   (attentive listening)

❏ *Happy Rhythms and Rhymes*
   Poem: "The Kangaroo" (page 23)
   Selected by: Patricia M. Cavanaugh
   (casual listening)

❏ *The Listening Walk*
   Author: Paul Showers
   (attentive listening)

❏ *Pano the Train*
   Author: Sharon Holanis
   (attentive listening)

Purpose

Skill L 35: listening for the main idea

❏ *Animals Should Definitely Not Wear Clothing* and *Animals Should Definitely Not Act Like People*
   Author: Judi Barrett
   Put construction paper over the covers so that the children can't see them. Read the story. Ask students to tell what the whole book was about.

❏ *The Berenstain Bears and the Prize Pumpkin*
   Authors: Stan and Jan Berenstain
   Father Bear's mind is taken off the true meaning of Thanksgiving in an effort to beat Farmer Ben at growing the largest pumpkin. By the end of the story, the Bears' minds are back on being thankful at Thanksgiving.

❏ *Good Books, Good Times!*
   Selected by: Lee Bennett Hopkins
   Read the poems in this book to students. Ask them to state what each poem is about. See if the overall idea—fun with books—is discovered.

❏ *Plants That Never Bloom*
   Author: Ruth Heller
   Conceal the book cover so students cannot see the title or cover illustrations. Read the story, sharing the illustrations. When the reading is completed, ask what the book was all about. This should produce the main idea.

❏ *Trees*
   Author: Ruth Thomson
   Cover the bold-faced headings. Read one page at a time. Ask students what all information on the page is about. This should produce the main idea.

Purpose (cont.)

Skill L 36: listening for details

❏ *The Bear Detectives*

Authors: Stan and Jan Berenstain

Children will need to listen to the details carefully to be able to solve the four mini-mysteries in this book.

❏ *Greyling*

Author: Jane Yolen

After hearing the story, the children should be able to tell about Greyling.

❏ *Strega Nona*

Author: Tomie dePaola

Children can listen for Strega Nona's magic words and also for which words Big Anthony neglects to use.

❏ *Whales: The Gentle Giants*

Author: Joyce Milton

Many facts about whales are revealed in this story. See if children can recall some of these details after hearing this story.

❏ *Where Fish Go in Winter and Answers to Other Great Mysteries*

Author: Amy Goldman Koss

The poems in this book present many facts and details about nature. See if children can remember the details after hearing these poems.

Skill L 37: listening for sequence

❏ *The Grouchy Ladybug*

Author: Eric Carle

This book uses sequencing in two ways. Clocks are shown on each page telling what time the ladybug visited each animal. The grouchy ladybug visits many animals, looking for one with which she can argue.

❏ *In the Forest*

Author: Marie Hall Ets

A little boy takes a walk in the forest. He imagines forest animals one at a time joining the walk. Children can listen to the story and then repeat in order the animals that joined the walk in the forest.

❏ *Ladybug, Ladybug*

Author: Ruth Brown

Children can listen for all of the stops that Ladybug makes on her way home to her children.

Purpose (cont.)

Skill L 37: listening for sequence (cont.)

❏ *Look . . . a Butterfly*

Author: David Cutts

After hearing this story, the children can tell the sequence of development of a butterfly.

❏ *The Very Busy Spider*

Author: Eric Carle

Many animals ask the spider to do something for them. See if the children can recall the animals and the task that each asked the spider to do.

Skill L 38: listening for cause and effect

❏ *The Giant Jam Sandwich*

Author: John Vernon Lord

A swarm of wasps invades the town of Itching Down. The wasps are such a nuisance that nobody wants to be outside. The town comes up with a clever way to rid themselves of the wasps. See if the children can name the effect of getting rid of the wasps.

❏ *Jumanji*

Author: Chris Van Allsburg

After hearing this story, children can recall what caused the animals to appear in Peter and Judy's house.

❏ *No Room for a Sneeze*

Author: Robyn Supraner

Have the students relate what causes the family to be peaceful and comfortable in the same living conditions with which they have previously been discontented.

❏ *Sylvester and the Magic Pebble*

Author: William Steig

Sylvester turns into a rock. See if the children can listen for the cause. The children can then state their own wishes.

❏ *What's in Fox's Sack?*

Author: Paul Galdone

Fox visits several houses and asks to leave his sack. He instructs the occupants of the house not to look in the sack. Curiosity causes each to look in the bag. Something happens to the original contents of the sack before Fox gets it back, so the occupants must give up something more valuable in return.

Purpose (cont.)

Skill L 39: listening for fact and opinion

❑ *Anatole*

Author: Eve Titus

Anatole the mouse becomes a cheese tester. He gives his opinion on how each cheese tastes and on how to improve the taste.

❑ *Christa McAuliffe: Reaching for the Stars*

Author: Patricia Stone Martin

Facts about astronaut-teacher Christa McAuliffe's life and death are presented in this simple biography.

❑ *Hansel and Gretel: The Witch's Story*

Author: Sheila Black

Children can share whether they agree with the witch's opinion or Hansel and Gretel's opinion of how the story really happened.

❑ *The Kids' Cat Book*

Author: Tomie dePaola

Many facts about cats, the care of cats, and the history of cats are presented in this book.

❑ *My New Boy*

Author: Joan Phillips

This story is told by a puppy. He believes that he is training the boy. The boy's opinion is that the puppy is being trained by him.

❑ *The True Story of the Three Little Pigs by A. Wolf*

Author: Jon Scieszka

Children can share which opinion they believe—the wolf's or the three pigs.

Skill L 40: understanding listening for entertainment

Any books that the teacher believes the students will enjoy listening to can be used to meet this objective.

Skill L 41: understanding that listening is a part of communication

❑ *Listen to Me*

Author: Barbara J. Neasi

A little boy learns the importance of listening to communicate. He practices what he has learned.

❑ *Television and Radio*

Author: Louis Sabin

Many forms of communication are discussed in this book. The importance of listening to communicate is stressed.

Techniques for Good Listening

Skill L 42: using good eye contact

This skill can be reinforced through the use of role-playing or creative dramatics. As children role-play or dramatize situations from books, they can use good eye contact by looking at the person to whom they are speaking.

Skills L 43: being aware of body language

❑ *Here Are My Hands*
Authors: Bill Martin, Jr. and John Archambault
The parts of the body are presented along with motions associated with each.

❑ *Thinking*
Authors: Kathie Billingslea Smith and Victoria Crenson
Various feelings and facial expressions are shown in the illustrations of this book.

❑ *What's It Like to Be a Puppeteer?*
Author: Susan Cornell Poskanzer
Facial expressions of the puppets and the puppeteers are discussed. Body language associated with working puppets is also presented.

Skill L 44: concentrating while listening

❑ *Animals Need Special Care*
Author: Dorothy Chlad
Children will need to concentrate while listening to this story so that they may relate facts about caring for animals. This would be a great book to read before a class pet comes.

❑ *Hand Rhymes*
Author: Marc Brown
The children will need to concentrate on the hand motions while they listen to the words of these entertaining fingerplays.

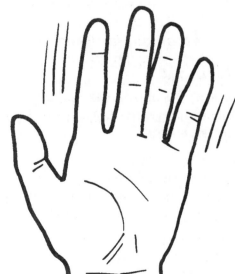

Skill L 44: concentrating while listening *(cont.)*

❑ *Lon Po Po*
Author: Ed Young
Before reading this story, ask the children to concentrate on the story to determine which well known fairy tale this tale is similar to.

❑ *Stories to Solve*
Author: George Shannon
Children will need to concentrate while listening to these mini-stories so that they will be able to answer the question or solve the problem at the end of the story.

Skill L 45: summarizing what has been listened to

Any book which holds the students' interests can be used.

Skill L 46: visualizing what has been listened to

❑ *A Big Fat Enormous Lie*
Author: Marjorie Weinman Sharmat
As a little boy's guilt about lying to his parents grows, the lie appears in the illustrations as an ugly monster. This monster grows and grows as the boy's conscience weighs more and more on him. When the boy tells the truth, the "lie" dies. The students can visualize their own "monster lie" as it grows and dies.

❑ *Follow the Drinking Gourd*
Author: Jeanette Winter
Children can visualize all of the places that the slaves go on the Underground Railroad.

❑ *Good Books, Good Times*
Poem: "I Met a Dragon Face to Face" (page 22)
Selected by: Lee Bennett Hopkins
Many descriptive words about the adventures one can find in a book are revealed here for children to visualize.

❑ *Something BIG Has Been Here*
Poem: "My Neighbor's Dog Is Purple" (page 41)
Author: Jack Prelutsky
A crocodile is visually described in this poem. After reading it aloud to children several times, have them draw the crocodile.

❑ *The Toy Circus*
Author: Jan Wahl
As a young boy dreams, his toy box becomes a circus tent. Have the children visualize each circus act as it is described in the book.

❑ *What If*
Author: Selma and Jack Wasserman
This book presents a series of "what if" questions. Children can visualize in their minds what item name they think answers the questions.

Phonetic Skills

Skill L 47: locating and identifying spelling patterns

The books listed below give many examples of words with common spelling patterns.

❏ *Bears on Wheels*
Authors: Stan and Jan Berenstain

❏ *George and Martha Round and Round*
Author: James Marshall

❏ *Good Books, Good Times*
Poem: "Give Me a Book" (page 13)
Selected by: Lee Bennett Hopkins

❏ *A New Treasury of Children's Poetry*
Poem: "The Last Cry of the Damp Fly" (page 96)
Poem: "Written in March" (page 143)
Selected by: Joanna Cole

Skill L 48: identifying and using r-controlled vowels

The poems listed below have examples of "r-controlled" vowels.

❏ *The New Kid on the Block*
Poem: "We Each Wore Half a Horse" (page 67)
Poem: "An Irritating Creature" (page 84)
Author: Jack Prelutsky

❏ *Something BIG Has Been Here*
Poem: "I'm Off to Catch a Bumblebee" (page 84)
Author: Jack Prelutsky

❏ *Zoo Doings*
Poem: "The Multilingual Mynah Bird" (page 16)
Author: Jack Prelutsky

❏ *A New Treasury of Children's Poetry*
Poem: "Southbound on the Freeway" (page 196)
Selected by: Joanna Cole

Phonetic Skills

Skill L 49: identifying vowel-consonant patterns

These books and poems present many common vowel-consonant patterns.

❑ *The Bear Detective*
  Authors: Stan and Jan Berenstain
❑ *Frog and Toad Are Friends*
  Author: Arnold Lobel
❑ *Good Books, Good Times*
  Poem: "I Met a Dragon Face to Face" (page 22)
  Selected by: Lee Bennett Hopkins
❑ *Happy Rhythms and Rhymes*
  Poem: "Listen" (page 9)
  Selected by: Patricia M. Cavanaugh
❑ *The New Kid on the Block*
  Poem: "Nine Mice" (page 9)
  Author: Jack Prelutsky

Dictionary Skills Objectives

Skill L 50: identifying and locating guide words and entry words

❑ *The Illustrated Flintstone Dictionary*
  Compiled by: Horace J. Elias
❑ *Sesame Street Dictionary*
  Author: Linda Hayward
❑ *Troll Student Encyclopedia*
  Authors: Michael Dempsey and Keith Lye

Skill L 51: locating and using illustrations

❑ *The Cat in the Hat Beginner's Dictionary*
  Author: P. D. Eastman
❑ *The Illustrated Flintstone Dictionary*
  Compiled by: Horace J. Elias
❑ *Letters, Sounds, and Words—A Phonic Dictionary*
  Author: Linda Hayward
❑ *Sesame Street Dictionary*
  Author: Linda Hayward

Visual Communication

Skill L 52: translating a story into pictures

❑ *Harold and the Purple Crayon*
Author: Crockett Johnson
After hearing this story, children can use their purple crayons to show how Harold got out of some of his jams.

❑ *It Happens to Everyone*
Author: Bernice Myers
A student and a teacher are featured preparing for the first day of school. Both have similar experiences. The students can draw pictures of an event from the book that relates to an experience that they have in preparing to start a new school year.

❑ *No, No, Joan*
Authors: Isaacsen, Bright and Margaret Holland
After hearing this story, children can draw pictures of three things that Joan did that her owner did not like.

❑ *Pumpkin, Pumpkin*
Author: Jeanne Titherington
Jamie plants a pumpkin seed. The story and illustrations show the development of the pumpkin. See if the children can show the development of the pumpkin in pictures.

❑ *Something BIG Has Been Here*
Poem: "They Never Send Sam to the Grocery Store" (page 78)
Author: Jack Prelutsky

Skill L 53: intepreting meanings of collages

The books listed below use collages as illustrations.

❑ *B Is for Bethlehem: A Christmas Alphabet*
Author: Isabel Wilner

❑ *In the Tall, Tall Grass*
Author: Denise Fleming

❑ *Spring*
Authors: Asun Balzola and Josep M. Parramon

❑ *Where the Forest Meets the Sea*
Author: Jeannie Baker

❑ *Window*
Author: Jeannie Baker

Locating and Using Information

> **Skill L 54: locating glossary, guide words, title page, table of contents, titles and subtitles, and chapter headings**

It is up to each individual teacher to find books that exhibit these qualities.

> **Skill L 55: alphabetizing words to the first letter**

❏ *Ed Emberley's A B C*
Author: Ed Emberley
This book is good as an introduction. The illustrations show letters of the alphabet being created. A word beginning with each letter is also presented. Discuss how letters and words are arranged in alphabetical order.

❏ *The Icky Bug Book and The Yucky Reptile Alphabet Book*
Author: Jerry Pallotta
Each letter of the alphabet features a reptile or bug name beginning with a specific letter. After sharing, children can name and alphabetize other creatures.

❏ *Science Dictionary of Animals*
Author: James Richardson
Animals are listed in alphabetical order in this book.

❏ *What Will I Be from A to Z*
Author: Donald L. Gelb
Careers are listed in alphabetical order. Children can add other occupations.

Organizing Information

> **Skill L 56: skimming for information**

❏ *Amazing Birds*
Author: Alexandra Parsons
A different bird is featured on each spread of pages. Photographs and illustrations give visual information about each bird. Small paragraphs are scattered around the pages. Children can skim the subtitles.

❏ *Amazing World of Plants*
Author: Elizabeth Marcus
The boldface headings help to make skimming easier for students.

❏ *Birds*
Author: Peter Gill
Boldface headings on each page make it easier to skim the pages.

❏ *Flowers*
Authors: Rosamund Kidman Cox and Barbara Cork
This book is divided into sections, each dealing with a different aspect or characteristic of flowers. Children can skim the topics and the sentences for needed information.

❏ *Strange Sea Creatures*
Author: Gina Ingoglia
Different types of sea creatures are introduced throughout this book. Each new creature's name is printed in bold type.

Reference Tools and Library Use

Skill L 57: being aware of a dictionary's use

❑ *Cat in the Hat Beginner's Dictionary*

By: P. D. Eastman

The entry words are listed alphabetically with a phrase or simple sentence using the entry word beneath. Illustrations appear for each word.

❑ *The Illustrated Flintstone Dictionary*

Compiled by: Horace J. Elias

Entry words are listed with definitions, tenses, and affixed versions of the word. Guide words are listed for the two-page spread. Not all entry words have illustrations.

❑ *Letters, Sounds, and Words—A Phonic Dictionary*

Author: Linda Hayward

This dictionary uses letters as guide words. Full-page illustrations show many words represented on the page.

❑ *Sesame Street Dictionary*

Author: Linda Hayward

Entry words are defined and used in complete sentences. Guide words and illustrations are included, too.

Skill L 58: being able to read and use simple graphs, maps, and charts

The books listed below give examples of simple graphs, maps, or charts. Each book is labeled to show which tool is represented within.

❑ *A Map Is a Picture*

Author: Barbara Rinkoff

(maps)

❑ *As the Crow Flies—A First Book of Maps*

Author: Gail Hartman

(maps)

❑ *How a Big Book Is Made*

Author: Aliki

(charts)

❑ *Ladybird First Facts About the Earth*

Author: Caroline Arnold

(maps, charts)

❑ *The Magic School Bus® Lost in the Solar System*

Author: Joanna Cole

(graph)

Lesson Plan

Date(s) _____

Skill(s)/Objective(s)

_____

_____

Resource(s)

_____

_____

_____

_____

Procedure

_____

_____

_____

_____

_____

_____

_____

Lesson Plan (cont.)

Procedure (cont.)

_____

_____

_____

_____

_____

_____

_____

_____

Application

_____

_____

_____

_____

_____

Notes/Comments

_____

_____

_____

_____

Skills Checklist

Skill	Skill Description	Completed (Check)	Notes
R 1	identifying words that rhyme		
R 2	developing eye, motor, voice control		
R 3	identifying a detail		
R 4	making inferences		
R 5	developing a sense of reading enjoyment		
R 6	reading Dolch words		
R 7	reading second-grade Thorndike words		
R 8	using words correctly in oral sentences		
R 9	using words correctly in written sentences		
R 10	recognizing meanings of words in context		
R 11	identifying some foreign words		
R 12	using figurative language in written and oral work		
R 13	using formal and informal language at appropriate times		

Skills Checklist (cont.)

Skill	Skill Description	Completed (Check)	Notes
R 14	identifying synonyms		
R 15	identifying antonyms		
R 16	identifying homophones, given two definitions		
R 17	using the context of illustrations to define a word		
R 18	using direct explanation to define a word		
R 19	using experience to define a word		
R 20	using mode or tone of voice		
R 21	using an example to define a word		
R 22	recognizing and comparing irregular plural nouns to singular nouns		
R 23	listening to and reproducing sounds		
R 24	listening to and identifying similar and different sounds		
R 25	identifying syllables heard in written and oral words		
R 26	matching consonant sounds		
R 27	matching consonant blends and digraphs		
R 28	matching vowels and vowel sounds		

Skills Checklist *(cont.)*

Skill	Skill Description	Completed (Check)	Notes
R 29	sounding out words beginning with consonant blends and digraphs		
R 30	sounding out one-syllable words with long vowel sounds		
R 31	sounding out one-syllable words with short vowel sounds		
R 32	sounding out one-syllable words with vowel combinations		
R 33	sounding out one-syllable words with digraphs		
R 34	building and using new words by using the same ending		
R 35	reading words with the same ending sounds		
R 36	identifying prefix, suffix, and root words		
R 37	reading and building compound words in affixed words		
R 38	reading and building contractions— apostrophe usage		
R 39	reading possessives—singular, plural, and apostrophe usage		
R 40	following stated directions		
R 41	recalling stated details		
R 42	identifying stated causes and effects in written material		
R 43	drawing conclusions implied in reading passages		

Skills Checklist *(cont.)*

Skill	Skill Description	Completed (Check)	Notes
R 44	comparing and contrasting ideas in reading selections		
R 45	stating a simplified analysis of character in a story		
R 46	demonstrating empathy with characters in a story		
R 47	summarizing a written passage		
R 48	stating the main idea in a written passage		
R 49	applying previously learned information to a new situation		
R 50	distinguishing facts from opinions in a story		
R 51	orally reading and interpreting sentences, using punctuation and phrasing		
R 52	demonstrating comprehension of material read silently		
R 53	identifying the stated main idea heard in a story		
R 54	recalling stated sequential events heard in a story		
R 55	selecting critical details heard in a story		
R 56	listening to and reading fiction stories		
R 57	listening to and reading nonfiction stories		
R 58	listening to and reading poetry		

Skills Checklist *(cont.)*

Skill	Skill Description	Completed (Check)	Notes
L 1	recognizing singular and plural nouns		
L 2	recognizing regular verbs in the past, present, and future tenses		
L 3	recognizing and using subject-verb agreement		
L 4	recognizing singular and plural personal pronouns		
L 5	recognizing polite pronoun order		
L 6	recognizing double negatives		
L 7	capitalizing the first word of a sentence		
L 8	capitalizing proper nouns		
L 9	capitalizing days of the week and months of the year		
L 10	capitalizing holidays		
L 11	capitalizing the personal pronoun "I"		
L 12	capitalizing titles before proper names		
L 13	capitalizing initials of persons' names		

Skills Checklist (cont.)

Skill	Skill Description	Completed (Check)	Notes
L 14	capitalizing parts of addresses		
L 15	using periods after declarative and imperative sentences		
L 16	using periods after numbers, initials, and abbreviations		
L 17	using commas to separate items in addresses		
L 18	using commas to separate items when writing the date		
L 19	using commas after the greeting and closing in personal letters		
L 20	using a question mark after an interrogative sentence		
L 21	using an exclamation point at the end of an exclamatory sentence		
L 22	writing a sentence using a simple subject and verb		
L 23	writing a sentence with agreement of subject and verb		
L 24	identifying the topic sentence of a paragraph		
L 25	writing a short creative composition		
L 26	writing poetry		
L 27	identifying heading, greeting, body, closing, and signature of a letter; arranging a letter neatly		
L 28	identifying the return address on an envelope; writing a block-style address on an envelope		
L 29	recognizing and using wordless picture books		
L 30	recognizing and using creative dramatics		
L 31	recognizing and using nursery rhymes		

Skills Checklist *(cont.)*

Skill	Skill Description	Completed (Check)	Notes
L 32	recognizing song		
L 33	recognizing rhyming endings in poetry		
L 34	distinguishing between casual and attentive listening		
L 35	listening for the main idea		
L 36	listening for details		
L 37	listening for sequence		
L 38	listening for cause and effect		
L 39	listening for fact and opinion		
L 40	understanding listening for entertainment		
L 41	understanding that listening is a part of communication		
L 42	using good eye contact		
L 43	being aware of body language		
L 44	concentrating while listening		
L 45	summarizing what has been listened to		

Skills Checklist *(cont.)*

Skill	Skill Description	Completed (Check)	Notes
L 46	visualizing what has been listened to		
L 47	locating and identifying spelling patterns		
L 48	identifying and using r-controlled vowels		
L 49	identifying vowel-consonant patterns		
L 50	identifying and locating guide words and entry words		
L 51	locating and using illustrations		
L 52	translating a story into pictures		
L 53	interpreting meanings of collages		
L 54	locating glossary, guide words, title page, table of contents, titles and subtitles, and chapter headings		
L 55	alphabetizing words to the first letter		
L 56	skimming for information		
L 57	being aware of a dictionary's use		
L 58	being able to read and use simple graphs, maps, and charts		

Additional Literature Appendix

Use this section for additional literature you may have available that reinforces the skills listed in this resource book. Reproduce copies as needed.

Skill

Book: _____

Author: _____

Summary: _____

_____

_____

_____

Skill

Book: _____

Author: _____

Summary: _____

_____

_____

_____

Skill

Book: _____

Author: _____

Summary: _____

_____

_____

Children's Literature References

Adler, David A. *A Picture Book of Benjamin Franklin.* Holiday House, 1990. (Canada: Thomas Allen & Son; UK & AUS: Baker & Taylor Int.)

Aliki. *At Mary Bloom's.* Greenwillow Books, 1976. (Canada: Gage Distributors; UK: International Book Distributors; AUS: Kirby Books)

————*How a Big Book Is Made.* Trumpet Club, 1990. (Canada & UK: Harper Collins Pub. Ltd.; AUS: Harper Collins)

————*The Story of Johnny Appleseed.* Trumpet Club, 1963. (Canada & UK: Harper Collins Pub. Ltd.; AUS: Harper Collins)

Allard, Harry. *Miss Nelson Is Missing.* Houghton Mifflin, 1977. (Canada: Thomas Allen & Son; UK: Cassell; AUS: Jackaranda Wiley)

Allen, Pamela. *Hidden Treasure.* G.P. Putnam's Sons, 1986. (Canada: BeJo Sales; UK & AUS: Warner International)

Allington, Richard. *Beginning to Learn About Opposites.* Raintree Children's Books, 1979. (Canada: Pippin; UK & AUS: Raintree)

Allinson, Beverly. *Effie.* Scholastic, 1990. (Canada: Scholastic; UK: Scholastic Limited; AUS: Ashton Scholastic Party Limited)

Anderson, J.I. *I Can Read About Whales and Dolphins.* Troll Associates, 1973. (Canada: Vanwell Pub.; UK & AUS: Penguin)

Anglund, Joan Walsh. *In a Pumpkin Shell.* Harcourt Brace Jovanovich, 1960. (Canada: HBJ; UK: HBJ (407) 345-3800; AUS:HBJ AUS)

Arnold, Caroline. *Ladybird First Facts About Animals.* Auburn: Ladybird Books, 1990.

————*Ladybird First Facts About the Earth.* Auburn: Ladybird Books, 1989.

Asch, Frank. *Happy Birthday, Moon.* Newfield Publications (date not available). Canada: Distican; UK: Simon & Schuster; AUS: Prentice Hall)

Baker, Jeannie. *Where the Forest Meets the Sea.* Greenwillow Books, 1987. (Canada: Gage Distributors; UK: International Book Distributors; AUS: Kirby Book Co.)

————*Window.* New York: Greenwillow Books, 1991. (Canada: Gage Distributors; UK: International Book Distributors; AUS: Kirby Book Co.)

Baker, Keith. *Hide and Snake.* Harcourt Brace Jovanovich, 1991. (Canada: HBJ; UK: HBJ (407) 345-3800; AUS: HBJ AUS)

Baker, Lucy. *Life in the Rainforest.* Scholastic, 1990. (Canada: Scholastic; UK: Scholastic Limited; AUS: Ashton Scholastic Party Limited)

Balzola, Asun and Josep M. Parramon. *Spring.* Children's Press, 1981. (Canada: Riverwood; AUS: Franklin Watts)

Banks, Kate. *Alphabet Soup.* Alfred A. Knopf, Inc., 1988. (Canada: Random House; UK: Random Century House; AUS: Random House)

Barrett, Judi. *Animals Should Definitely Not Act Like People.* Scholastic, 1980. (Canada: Scholastic; UK: Scholastic Limited; AUS: Ashton Scholastic Party Limited)

————*Animals Should Definitely Not Wear Clothing.* Scholastic, 1970. (Canada:Scholastic; UK: Scholastic Limited; AUS: Ashton Scholastic Party Limited)

Children's Literature References *(cont.)*

Barrett, Judi. *Cloudy with a Chance of Meatballs*. Houghton, 1989. (Canada: Thomas Allen & Son; UK: Cassell; AUS: Jackaranda Wiley)

Barrett, Judith. *Old MacDonald Had an Apartment House*. Atheneum, 1969. (Canada: Distican; UK: Simon & Schuster; AUS: Prentice Hall)

————*A Snake Is Totally Tail*. Atheneum, 1983. (Canada: Distican; UK: Simon & Schuster; AUS: Prentice Hall)

————*The Wind Thief*. Atheneum, 1977. (Canada: Distican; UK: Simon & Schuster; AUS: Prentice Hall)

Bass, Marilyn & Marvin Goldman. *Growing Wild*. Macmillan, 1975. (Canada: Distican; UK: Simon & Schuster; AUS: Prentice Hall)

Battaglia, Aurelius. *Seasons*. Platt & Mune, 1977.

Baylor, Byrd. *Hawk, I'm Your Brother*. Macmillan, 1976. (Canada: Distican; UK: Simon & Schuster; AUS: Prentice Hall)

————*When Clay Sings*. Charles Scribner's Sons, 1972. (Canada: Distican; UK: Simon & Schuster; AUS: Prentice Hall)

Behrens, June. *The Manners Book*. Children's Press, 1980. (Canada: Riverwood Press; AUS: Franklin Watts)

Benchley, Nathaniel. *Sam the Minuteman*. Scholastic, 1969. (Canada: Scholastic; UK: Scholastic Limited; AUS: Ashton Scholastic Party Limited)

Bennett, Jill. *Teeny Tiny*. Trumpet, 1985.

Berenstain, Stan and Jan. *The Bear Detectives*. Random House, 1975. (Canada & AUS: Random House; UK: Random Century House)

————*Bears in the Night*. Random House, 1971. (Canada & AUS: Random House; UK: Random Century House)

————*Bears on Wheels*. Random House, 1969. (Canada & AUS: Random House; UK: Random Century House)

————*The Berenstain Bears Get in a Fight*. Random House, 1982. (Canada & AUS: Random House; UK: Random Century House)

————*C Is for Clown*. Random House, 1972. (Canada & AUS: Random House; UK: Random Century House)

————*The Berenstain Bears Don't Pollute (Anymore)*. Random House, 1991. (Canada & AUS: Random House; UK: Random Century House)

————*Old Hat, New Hat*. Random House, 1970. (Canada & AUS: Random House; UK: Random Century House)

————*On the Moon*. Random House, 1985. (Canada & AUS: Random House; UK: Random Century House)

————*The Berenstain Bears and the Prize Pumpkin*. Random House, 1980. (Canada & AUS: Random House; UK: Random Century House)

————*The Bears' Vacation*. Random House, 1968. (Canada & AUS: Random House; UK: Random Century House)

Berenstain, Stanley and Janice. *The Berenstains' B Book*. Random House, 1971. (Canada & AUS: Random House; UK: Random Century House)

Bester, Roger. *Guess What*. Crown Publishers, Inc., 1980. (Canada & AUS: Random House; UK: Random Century House)

Bider, Djemma. *The Biggest Little House in the Forest*. Caedmon, 1986.

Children's Literature References *(cont.)*

Billingslea, Kathie and Victoria Creson. *Thinking*. Troll, 1988. (Canada: Vanwell Pub.; UK: Penguin; AUS: Penguin AUS)

Black, Sheila. *Hansel and Gretel: The Witch's Story*. Carol Publishing, 1991.

Blake, Robert J. *The Perfect Spot*. Philomel Books, 1992. (Canada: BeJo Sales; UK & AUS: Warner International)

Blume, Judy. *The One in the Middle Is the Green Kangaroo*. Bradbury Press, 1981. (Canada: Doubleday Dell Seal; UK: Bantam Doubleday Dell; AUS: Transworld Publishers)

Bond, Michael. *Paddington's Opposites*. Viking, 1990. (Canada: Penguin Books Can.; UK: Penguin UK; AUS: Penguin Books AUS)

Bourne, Miriam Anne. *Let's Visit a Toy Factory*. Troll, 1988. (Canada: Vanwell Pub.; UK & AUS: Penguin)

Brandt, Keith. *What Makes It Rain? The Story of a Raindrop*. Troll, 1982. (Canada: Vanwell Pub.; UK & AUS: Penguin)

Brett, Jan. *Annie and the Wild Animals*. Houghton Mifflin Co., 1985. (Canada: Thomas Allen & Son; UK: Cassell; AUS: Jackaranda Wiley)

————*The Twelve Days of Christmas*. Trumpet Club, 1986. (Canada: BeJo Sales; UK & AUS: Warner International)

Bridwell, Norman. *Clifford the Big Red Dog*. Scholastic, 1985. (Canada: Scholastic; UK: Scholastic Limited; AUS: Ashton Scholastic Party Limited)

————*Clifford's Family*. Scholastic, 1984. (Canada: Scholastic; UK: Scholastic Limited; AUS: Ashton Scholastic Party Limited)

————*Clifford's Pals*. Scholastic, 1985. (Canada: Scholastic; UK: Scholastic Limited; AUS: Ashton Scholastic Party Limited)

————*Clifford's Word Book*. Scholastic, 1990. (Canada: Scholastic; UK: Scholastic Limited; AUS: Ashton Scholastic Party Limited)

Briggs, Raymond. *Jim and the Beanstalk*. Coward-McCann, Inc., 1970. (Canada: BeJo Sales; UK & AUS: Warner International)

Bright, Isaacsen & Margaret Holland. *No, No, Joan*. School Book Fairs, 1983.

Brown, Craig. *My Barn*. Greenwillow Books, 1991. (Canada: Gage Distributors; UK: International Book Distributors; AUS: Kirby Book Co.)

Brown, Marc. *Arthur's Thanksgiving*. The Trumpet Club, 1983. (Canada: Little Brown; UK: Little Brown Ltd.; AUS: Penguin)

————*Hand Rhymes*. E.P. Dutton, 1985. (Canada: Little Brown; AUS: Penguin Books AUS; UK: Penguin UK)

Brown, Margaret Wise. *The Runaway Bunny*. HarperCollins, 1942. (Canada & UK: HarperCollins Pub. Ltd.; AUS: HarperCollins)

Brown, Ruth. *A Dark, Dark Tale*. Dial Books for Young Children, 1981. (Canada: Penguin Books CAN; AUS: Penguin Books AUS; UK: Penguin)

————*Ladybug, Ladybug*. E. P. Dutton, 1980. (Canada: Penguin Books CAN; AUS: Penguin Books AUS; UK: Penguin)

————*The Big Sneeze*. Lothrop, Lee & Shepard Books, 1985. (Canada: Gage Distributors; UK: International Book Distributors; AUS: Kirby Book Co.)

Buchanan, Heather S. *George and Matilda Mouse and the Floating School*. Simon & Schuster, Inc., 1990. (Canada: Distican; UK: Simon & Schuster; AUS: Prentice Hall)

Bulla, Clyde Robert. *Pocahontas and the Strangers*. Scholastic, 1971. (Canada: Scholastic; UK: Scholastic Limited; AUS: Ashton Scholastic Party Limited)

Children's Literature References *(cont.)*

Burton, Virginia Lee. *The Little House.* Houghton Mifflin Co., 1942. (Canada: Thomas Allen & Son; UK: Cassell; AUS: Jackaranda Wiley)

Calmenson, Stephanie. *What Am I?* Harper & Row, 1989. (Canada & UK: HarperCollins Pub. Ltd.; AUS: HarperCollins)

Cameron, Polly. *'I Can't', Said the Ant."* Scholastic, 1961. (Canada: Scholastic; UK: Scholastic Limited; AUS: Ashton Scholastic Party Limited)

Carle, Eric. *A House for Hermit Crab.* Saxonville Picture Book Studios, 1987. (Canada: Distican; UK: Simon & Schuster; AUS: Prentice Hall)

————*Pancakes, Pancakes.* Saxonville Picture Book Studio, 1990. (Canada: Distican; UK: Simon & Schuster; AUS: Prentice Hall)

————*The Grouchy Ladybug.* Harper & Row, 1977. (Canada & UK: HarperCollins Pub. Ltd.; AUS: HarperCollins)

————*The Mixed-Up Chameleon.* HarperCollins, 1975. (Canada & UK: HarperCollins Pub. Ltd.; AUS: HarperCollins)

————*The Secret Birthday Message.* HarperCollins, 1972. (Canada & UK: HarperCollins Pub. Ltd.; AUS: HarperCollins)

————*The Very Busy Spider.* Philomel Books, 1984. (Canada: BeJo Sales; UK & AUS: Warner Int.)

————*The Very Hungry Caterpillar.* Philomel Books, 1987. (Canada: BeJo Sales; UK & AUS: Warner Int.)

————*The Very Quiet Cricket.* Philomel Books, 1990. (Canada: BeJo Sales; UK & AUS: Warner Int.)

Carlstrom, Nancy White. *Better Not Get Wet, Jesse Bear.* Macmillan, 1988. (Canada: Distican; UK: Simon & Schuster; AUS: Prentice Hall)

Carrick, Carol. *What Happened to Patrick's Dinosaurs?* Trumpet Club, 1986. (Canada: Thomas Allen & Son; UK: Cassell; AUS: Jackaranda Wiley)

Caseley, Judith. *Dear Annie.* Greenwillow, 1991. (Canada: Gage Distributors; UK: International Book Distributors; AUS: Kirby Book Co.)

Cauley, Lorinda Bryan. *Clap Your Hands.* G. P. Putnam's Sons, 1992. (Canada: BeJo Sales; UK & AUS: Warner Int.)

Cavanaugh, Patricia M. *Happy Rhythms and Rhymes.* American Education, 1971.

Chartier, Normand. *Over the River and Through the Woods.* Simon & Schuster, 1987. (Canada: Distican; UK: Simon & Schuster; AUS: Prentice Hall)

Cherry, Lynne. *The Great Kapok Tree.* Harcourt Brace Jovanovich, 1990. (Canada & UK: HBJ; AUS: HBJ AUS)

Chlad, Dorothy. *Animals Need Special Care.* Weekly Reader Books, 1985.

————*Strangers.* Regensteiner Publishing, 1982. (Canada: Riverwood; AUS: Franklin Watts)

Cohen, Barbara. *Molly's Pilgrim.* Bantam Skylark Books, 1983. (Canada: Doubleday Dell Seal; UK: Bantam Doubleday Dell; AUS: Transworld Pub.)

Cole, Joanna. *A New Treasury of Children's Poetry.* New York: Doubleday, 1984. (Canada: Doubleday Dell Seal; UK: Bantam Doubleday Dell; AUS: Transworld Pub.)

————*The Magic School Bus® Lost in the Solar System.* Scholastic, 1990. (Canada: Scholastic; UK: Scholastic Limited; AUS: Ashton Scholastic Party Limited)

Children's Literature References *(cont.)*

Cole, Sheila. *When the Rain Stops*. Lothrop, Lee & Shepard Books, 1991. (Canada: Gage Distributors; UK: International Book Distributors; AUS: Kirby Book Co.)

Coletta, Irene and Hallie. *From A to Z*. Prentice Hall, 1979. (Canada: Distican; UK: Simon & Schuster; AUS: Prentice Hall)

Cooney, Barbara. *Miss Rumphius*. Viking Press, 1982. (Canada: Penguin Bks Can; UK: Penguin UK; AUS: Penguin Bks AUS)

Cosgrove, Stephen. *Rhubarb*. Price Stern Sloan, 1988. (Canada: BeJo Sales; UK & AUS: Warner International)

Cox, Rosamund Kidman and Barbara Cork. *Flowers*. EDC Publishing, 1980.

Cutts, David. *Look . . . a Butterfly*. Troll Associates, 1982. (Canada: Vanwell Pub.; UK & AUS: Penguin Bks)

Dabcovich, Lydia. *Mrs. Huggins and Her Hen Hannah*. E. P. Dutton, 1985. (AUS: Penguin Books AUS; UK: Penguin UK)

Daugherty, James. *The Landing of the Pilgrims*. Random House, 1950. (Canada & AUS: Random House; UK: Random Century House)

Day, Alexandra. *Carl's Afternoon in the Park*. Farrar & Straus & Giroux, 1991. (Canada: HarperCollins; UK: Victor Gollancz; AUS: Jackaranda Wiley)

————*Good Dog, Carl*. Green Tiger Press, 1985. (Canada: General Pub.; UK: International Book Dist.; AUS: Simon & Schuster)

Degen, Bruce. *Jamberry*. Scholastic, 1983. (Canada: Scholastic; UK: Scholastic Limited; AUS: Ashton Scholastic Party Limited)

Delacre, Lulu. *Nathan and Nicholas Alexander*. Scholastic Inc., 1986. (Canada: Scholastic; UK: Scholastic Limited; AUS: Ashton Scholastic Party Limited)

Demi. *Demi's Find the Animal ABC*. The Trumpet Club, 1985. (Canada: BeJo Sales; UK & AUS: Warner International)

————*The Empty Pot*. Trumpet Club, 1990. (Canada: Fitz Henry & Whiteside; UK: Pan Demic Limited; AUS: CIS Publishers)

Dempsey, Michael and Keith Lye. *Troll Student Encyclopedia*. Troll, 1991. (Canada: Vanwell Pub.; UK & AUS: Penguin Bks)

Dennis, Wesley. *Flip*. Penguin Books, 1941. (Canada: Penguin Bks Can; UK: Penguin UK; AUS: Penguin Bks AUS)

dePaola, Tomie. *Andy: That's My Name*. Prentice Hall, 1973. (Canada: Distican; UK: Simon & Schuster; AUS: Prentice Hall)

————*The Hunter and the Animals*. Holiday House, 1981. (Canada: Thomas Allen & Son; UK & AUS: Baker & Taylor Int.)

————*Strega Nona*. Prentice Hall Books for Young Readers, 1975. (Canada: Distican; UK: Simon & Schuster; AUS: Prentice Hall)

————*The Kids' Cat Book*. Trumpet Club, 1979. (Canada: Thomas Allen & Son; UK & AUS: Baker & Taylor Int.)

Domanska, Janina. *The Turnip*. Macmillan, 1969. (Canada: Distican; UK: Simon & Schuster; AUS: Prentice Hall)

Donnelly, Judy. *A Wall of Names*. Random, 1991. (Can & AUS: Random House; UK: Random Century House)

Dunbar, Joyce. *Ten Little Mice*. Harcourt Brace Jovanovich, 1990. (Canada & UK: HBJ; AUS: HBJ AUS)

Children's Literature References *(cont.)*

Duncan, Lois. *The Birthday Moon*. Viking Kestrel, 1989. (Canada: Penguin Bks Can; UK: Penguin UK; AUS: Penguin Bks AUS)

Dunrea, Olivier. *Deep Down Underground*. Macmillan, 1989. (Canada: Distican; UK: Simon & Schuster; AUS: Prentice Hall)

Dupasquier, Philippe. *Our House on the Hill*. Viking Press, 1987. (Canada: Penguin Bks Can; UK: Penguin UK; AUS: Penguin Bks AUS)

Eastman, P. D. *The Cat in the Hat Beginner's Dictionary*. Random House, 1964. (Canada & AUS: Random House; UK: Random Century House)

————*Are You My Mother?* Random House, 1960. (Canada & AUS: Random House; UK: Random Century House)

————*Go Dog Go!* Random House, 1961. (Canada & AUS: Random House; UK: Random Century House)

Ehlert, Lois. *Circus*. HarperCollins, 1992. (Canada & UK: HarperCollins Pub. Ltd.; AUS: HarperCollins)

————*Color Farm*. J. B. Lippincott, 1990. (UK: Peter Gemmel)

Eisen, Armand (retold by). *Goldilocks and the Three Bears*. Alfred A. Knopf, Inc., 1987. (Canada: Penguin Books Can; UK: Dorling Kindersley; AUS: HarperCollins)

Ekker, Ernst A. *What Is Beyond the Hill?* J.B. Lippincott, 1985. (UK: Peter Gemmel)

Elias, Horace J. *The Illustrated Flintstone Dictionary*. Ottenheimer, 1979.

Elswit, Sharon. *Animal Homes*. Western Publishing Company Inc., 1984. (Canada & UK: Western Pub. Inc.; AUS: Golden Press Party Ltd.)

Elting, Mary & Michael Folsom. *Q Is for Duck*. Clarion Books, 1980. (Canada: Thomas Allen & Son; UK: Cassell; AUS: Jackaranda Wiley)

Emberley, Edward. *Ed Emberley's ABC*. Little, Brown & Co., 1978. (Canada: Little Brown; UK: Little Brown Ltd.; AUS: Penguin)

Ets, Marie Hall and Aurora Labstida. *Nine Days to Christmas*. Viking, 1959. (Canada: Penguin Bks Can; UK: Penguin UK; AUS: Penguin Bks AUS)

Flack, Marjorie. *Angus and the Cat*. Doubleday, 1931. (Canada: Doubleday Dell Seal; UK: Bantam Doubleday Dell; AUS: Transworld Pub.)

Fleming, Denise. *In the Tall, Tall Grass*. Henry Holt and Company, 1991. (Canada: Fitz Henry & Whiteside; UK: Pan Demic Limited; AUS: CIS Pub.)

Freeman, Don. *Corduroy*. Viking Press, 1968. (Canada: Penguin Bks Can; UK: Penguin UK; AUS: Penguin Bks AUS)

Frith, Michael. *I'll Teach My Dog 100 Words*. Random House, 1973. (Canada & AUS: Random House; UK: Random Century House)

Frost, Erica. *I Can Read About Good Manners*. Troll Associates, 1975. (Canada: Penguin Bks Can; UK: Penguin UK; AUS: Penguin Bks AUS)

————*Mystery of the Runaway Sled*. Troll Associates, 1979. (Canada: Penguin Bks Can; UK: Penguin UK; AUS: Penguin Bks AUS)

Gackenbach, Dick. *Hound and Bear*. The Seabury Press, 1976.

Children's Literature References *(cont.)*

Galdone, Joanna. *The Little Girl and the Big Bear*. Houghton Mifflin, 1980. (Canada: Thomas Allen & Son; UK: Cassell; AUS: Jackaranda Wiley)

Galdone, Paul. *Over in the Meadow*. Prentice Hall Books for Young Readers, 1986. (Canada: Distican; UK: Simon & Schuster; AUS: Prentice Hall)

————*What's in Fox's Sack?* Clarion Books, 1982. (Canada: Thomas Allen & Son; UK: Cassell; AUS: Jackaranda Wiley)

Gammell, Stephen. *Once upon MacDonald's Farm*. Macmillan Publishing, 1981. (Canada: Distican; UK: Simon & Schuster; AUS: Prentice Hall)

Garelick, May. *What's Inside*. William R. Scott (date not available).

Gelb, Donald. *What Will I Be from A to Z*. National Dairy Council, 1973.

Gibbons, Gail. *From Seed to Plant*. Holiday House, 1991. (Canada: Thomas Allen & Son; UK & AUS: Baker & Taylor Int.)

————*Paper, Paper Everywhere*. Harcourt Brace Jovanovich, 1983. (Canada & UK: HBJ; AUS: HBJ AUS)

Giganti, Paul, Jr. *Each Orange Has 8 Slices: A Counting Book*. Greenwillow Books, 1992. (Canada: Gage Distributors; UK: International Book Distributors; AUS: Kirby Book Co.

Gilman, Phoebe. *The Wonderful Pigs of Jillian Jiggs*. Scholastic, 1988. (Canada: Scholastic; UK: Scholastic Limited; AUS: Ashton Scholastic Party Limited)

Goennel, Heidi. *If I Were a Penguin*. Little, Brown, and Company, 1989. (Canada: Little Brown; UK: Little Brown Ltd.; AUS: Penguin)

Guarino, Deborah. *Is Your Mama a Llama?* Scholastic, Inc., 1989. (Canada: Scholastic; UK: Scholastic Limited; AUS: Ashton Scholastic Party Limited)

Gwynne, Fred. *A Chocolate Moose for Dinner*. The Trumpet Club, 1976. (Canada: Distican; UK: Simon & Schuster; AUS: Prentice Hall)

————A *Little Pigeon Toad*. The Trumpet Club, 1988. (Canada: Distican; UK: Simon & Schuster; AUS: Prentice Hall)

————*The King Who Rained*. Simon & Schuster, 1970. (Canada: Distican; UK: Simon & Schuster; AUS: Prentice Hall)

————*The Sixteen Hand Horse*. New York: Simon & Schuster, 1980. (Canada: Distican; UK: Simon & Schuster; AUS: Prentice Hall)

Hader, Berta and Elmer. *The Big Snow*. Macmillan, 1948. (Canada: Distican; UK: Simon & Schuster; AUS: Prentice Hall)

————*The Mighty Hunter*. New York: Scholastic, 1943. (Canada: Scholastic; UK: Scholastic Limited; AUS: Ashton Scholastic Party Limited)

Hall, Donald. *The Ox-Cart Man*. The Viking Press, 1979. (Canada: Penguin Bks Can; UK: Penguin UK; AUS: Penguin Bks AUS)

Hanson, Joan. *Antonyms*. Lerner Publications, 1972. (Canada: Riverwood Pub.; UK: Turnaround; AUS: Stafford Books)

————*Homographs*. Lerner Publications, 1972. (Canada: Riverwood Pub.; UK: Turnaround; AUS: Stafford Books)

————*More Antonyms*. Lerner Publications, 1973. (Canada: Riverwood Pub.; UK: Turnaround; AUS: Stafford Books)

Children's Literature References *(cont.)*

Hanson, Joan. *More Synonyms*. Lerner Publications, 1973. (Canada: Riverwood Pub.; UK: Turnaround; AUS: Stafford Books)

———*Sound Words*. Lerner Publications, 1976. (Canada: Riverwood Pub.; UK: Turnaround; AUS: Stafford Books)

———*Still More Antonyms*. Lerner Publications, 1976. (Canada: Riverwood Pub.; UK: Turnaround; AUS: Stafford Books)

———*Still More Synonyms*. Lerner Publications, 1973. (Canada: Riverwood Pub.; UK: Turnaround; AUS: Stafford Books)

———*Synonyms*. Lerner Publications, 1976. (Canada: Riverwood Pub. UK: Turnaround; AUS: Stafford Books)

Harshman, Marc. *A Little Excitement*. Cobblehill Books, 1989. (Canada: Penguin Bks Can; AUS: Penguin Books AUS; UK: Penguin)

———*Snow Company*. Cobblehill Books, 1990. (Canada: Penguin Bks Can; AUS: Penguin Books AUS; UK: Penguin)

Hartman, Gail. *As the Crow Flies*. Bradbury Press, 1991. (Canada: Doubleday Dell Seal; UK: Bantam Doubleday Dell; AUS: Transworld Publishers)

Hawkins, Colin and Jacqui. *Zug the Bug*. G. P. Putnam's Sons, 1988. (Canada: BeJo Sales; UK & AUS: Warner International)

Hayward, Linda. *Letters, Sounds, and Words—A Phonic Dictionary*. Platt & Munk, 1973.

———*Sesame Street Dictionary*. Random House, 1980. (Canada & AUS: Random House; UK: Random Century House)

Heiligman, Deborah. *Into the Night*. Harper & Row, 1990. (Canada & UK: HarperCollins Pub. Ltd.; AUS: HarperCollins)

Heller, Ruth. *Chickens Aren't the Only Ones*. Grosset & Dunlap, 1981. (Canada: BeJo Sales; UK & AUS: Warner International)

———*Kites Sail High*. New York: Grosset & Dunlap, 1988. (Canada: BeJo Sales; UK & AUS: Warner International)

———*Many Luscious Lollipops*. Grosset & Dunlap, 1989. (Canada: BeJo Sales; UK & AUS: Warner International)

———*Merry-Go-Round*. Grosset & Dunlap, 1990. (Canada: BeJo Sales; UK & AUS: Warner International)

———*Plants That Never Ever Bloom*. Scholastic, 1984. (Canada: Scholastic; UK: Scholastic Limited, AUS: Ashton Scholastic Party Limited)

———*The Reason for a Flower*. Grosset & Dunlap, 1983. Canada: BeJo Sales; UK & AUS: Warner International)

Henkes, Kevin. *Chester's Way*. Greenwillow Books, 1988. (Canada: Gage Distributors; UK: International Book Distributors; AUS: Kirby Book Co.)

———*Chrysanthemum*. Trumpet, 1991. (Canada: Gage Distributors; UK: International Book Distributors; AUS: Kirby Book Co.)

———*Grandpa and Bo*. Greenwillow Books, 1986. (Canada: Gage Distributors; UK: International Book Distributors; AUS: Kirby Book Co.)

Hennessy, B. G. *Jake Baked the Cake*. Viking, 1990. (Canada: Penguin Bks Can; UK: Penguin UK; AUS: Penguin Bks AUS)

Children's Literature References *(cont.)*

Hines, Anna Grossnickle. *Remember the Butterflies*. Dutton Children's Press, 1991. (Canada: Penguin Bks Can; AUS: Penguin Bks AUS; UK: Penguin UK)

Hoban, Russell. *Best Friends for Frances*. Harper & Row, 1969. (Canada & UK: HarperCollins Publishers Ltd.; AUS: HarperCollins)

Hoban, Tana. *Big Ones, Little Ones*. Greenwillow Books, 1976. (Canada: Gage Distributors; UK: International Book Distributors; AUS: Kirby Book Co.)

————*Exactly the Opposite*. New York: Greenwillow Books, 1990. (Canada: Gage Distributors; UK: International Book Distributors; AUS: Kirby Book Co.)

————*Is It Larger? Is It Smaller?* Greenwillow Books, 1985. (Canada: Gage Distributors; UK: International Book Distributors; AUS: Kirby Book Co.)

————*Is It Rough? Is It Smooth? Is It Shiny?* Greenwillow Books, 1984. (Canada: Gage Distributors; UK: International Book Dist.; AUS: Kirby Book Co.)

————*Look Again!* Macmillan, 1971. (Canada: Distican; UK: Simon & Schuster; AUS: Prentice Hall)

————*Look! Look! Look!* Greenwillow Books, 1988. (Canada: Gage Distributors; UK: International Book Dist.; AUS: Kirby Book Co.)

————*Push, Pull, Empty, Full*. Macmillan, 1972. (Canada: Distican; UK: Simon & Schuster; AUS: Prentice Hall)

Hoberman, Mary Ann. *A House Is a House for Me*. Viking Press, 1978. (Canada: Penguin Books Can; UK: Penguin UK; AUS: Penguin Books AUS)

Holanis, Sharon. *Pano the Train*. Western Publishing Company, 1975.

Holroyd, Angela. *The Lost Present*. Gallery Books, 1990.

Hooks, William H. *A Dozen Dizzy Dogs*. Bantam Books, 1990. (Canada: Doubleday Dell Seal; UK: Bantam Doubleday Dell; AUS: Transworld Pub.)

Hopkins, Lee Bennett. *Good Books, Good Times*. Macmillan Publishing, 1972. (Canada & UK: HarperCollins Publishers Ltd.; AUS: HarperCollins)

Hutchins, Pat. *One Hunter*. Greenwillow Books, 1982. (Canada: Gage Distributors; UK: International Book Dist.; AUS: Kirby Book Co.)

————*The Doorbell Rang*. Greenwillow Books, 1986. (Canada: Gage Distributors; UK: International Book Dist.; AUS: Kirby Book Co.)

————*Good-Night, Owl!* Macmillan Publishing, 1972. (Canada: Distican; UK: Simon & Schuster; AUS: Prentice Hall)

————*The Wind Blew*. Macmillan, 1974. (Canada: Distican; UK: Simon & Schuster; AUS: Prentice Hall)

————*Which Witch Is Which?* Greenwillow Books, 1989. (Canada: Gage Distributors; UK: International Book Dist.; AUS: Kirby Book Co)

Ingoglia, Gina. *Strange Sea Creatures*. Western Publishing, 1991.

Jeunesse, Gallimard, & Pascale de Bourgoing. *Weather*. Scholastic, 1991. (Canada: Scholastic; UK: Scholastic Limited; AUS: Ashton Scholastic Party Limited)

Children's Literature References *(cont.)*

Johnson, Crockett. *Harold and the Purple Crayon.* Harper & Row, 1955. (Canada & UK: HarperCollins Pub. Ltd.; AUS: HarperCollins)

Jonas, Ann. *Round Trip.* Scholastic, 1983. (Canada: Scholastic; UK: Scholastic Limited; AUS: Ashton Scholastic Party Limited)

————*The Trek.* Greenwillow Books, 1975. (Canada: Gage Distributors; UK: International Book Dist.; AUS: Kirby Book Co)

Keats, Ezra Jack. *Pet Show!* Macmillan, 1972. (Canada: Distican; UK: Simon & Schuster; AUS: Prentice Hall)

————*Peter's Chair.* HarperCollins, 1967. (Canada & UK: HarperCollins Pub. Ltd.; AUS: HarperCollins)

————*The Snowy Day.* Scholastic, Inc., 1962. (Canada: Scholastic; UK: Scholastic Limited; AUS: Ashton Scholastic Party Limited)

Kellogg, Steven. *Best Friends.* Dial Books for Young Readers, 1986. (Canada: Penguin Books Can; UK: Penguin UK; AUS: Penguin Books AUS)

Kitchen, Bert. *Pig in a Barrow.* Dial Books for Young Readers, 1991. (Canada: Penguin Books Can; UK: Penguin UK; AUS: Penguin Books AUS)

Klasky, Charles. *Rugs Have Naps (But Never Take Them).* Children's Press, 1984. (Canada: Riverwood; AUS: Franklin Watts)

Klein, Monica. *Backyard Basketball Superstar.* Pantheon Books, 1981. (Canada & AUS: Random House; UK: Random Century House)

Krauss, Ruth. *The Carrot Seed.* Harper & Row, 1945. (Canada & UK: HarperCollins Pub. Ltd.; AUS: HarperCollins)

————*A Very Special House.* Harper & Row, 1953. (Canada & UK: HarperCollins Pub. Ltd.; AUS: HarperCollins)

Kroll, Steven. *Oh, What a Thanksgiving!* Scholastic, 1988. (Canada: Scholastic; UK: Scholastic Limited; AUS: Ashton Scholastic Party Limited

————*Princess Abigail and the Wonderful Hat.* Holiday House, 1991. (Canada: Thomas Allen & Son; UK & AUS: Baker & Taylor Int.)

Kudrna, C. Imbior. *Two-Way Words.* Abingdon, 1980.

Larche, Dr. Douglas W. *Father Gander Nursery Rhymes.* Santa Barbara: Advocacy, 1985.

Larrick, Nancy. *More Poetry for Holidays.* Scholastic, 1973. (Canada: Scholastic; UK: Scholastic Limited; AUS: Ashton Scholastic Party Limited)

Leodhas, Sorche Nic. *Always Room for One More.* Henry Holt and Co., 1965. (Canada: Fitz Henry & Whiteside; UK: Pan Demic Ltd.; AUS: CIS Pub.)

Le Sieg, Theo. *The First of October.* Random, 1977. (Canada & AUS: Random House; UK: Random Century House)

————*Hooper Humperdink . . . ? Not Him.* Random House, 1976. (Canada & AUS: Random House; UK: Random Century House)

————*In a People House.* Random, 1972. (Canada & AUS: Random House; UK: Random Century House)

————*Maybe You Should Fly a Jet! Maybe You Should Be a Vet!* Random House, 1980. (Canada & AUS: Random House; UK: Random Century House)

————*The Tooth Book.* Random House, 1981. (Canada & AUS: Random House; UK: Random Century House)

Children's Literature References *(cont.)*

Le Sieg, Theo. *Would You Rather Be a Bullfrog?* Random House, 1975. (Canada & AUS: Random House; UK: Random Century House)

Levarie, Norma. *I Had a Little . . .* Random House, 1961. (Canada & AUS: Random House; UK: Random Century House)

Levine, Ellen. *If You Traveled West in a Covered Wagon.* Scholastic, 1992. (Canada: Scholastic; UK: Scholastic Limited; AUS: Ashton Scholastic Party Limited)

Lionni, Leo. *A Flea Story.* Pantheon, 1977. (Canada: Random House; UK: Random Century House; AUS: Random House Party Limited)

————*Alexander and the Wind-up Mouse.* New York: Scholastic, 1969. (Canada: Scholastic; UK: Scholastic Limited; AUS: Ashton Scholastic Party Limited)

————*The Alphabet Tree.* The Trumpet Club, 1968. (Canada: Distican; UK: Simon & Schuster; AUS: Prentice Hall)

————*Swimmy.* New York: Scholastic, 1963. (Canada: Scholastic; UK: Scholastic Limited; AUS: Ashton Scholastic Party Limited)

Littledale, Freya. *The Snow Child.* Scholastic, 1978. (Canada: Scholastic; UK: Scholastic Limited; AUS: Ashton Scholastic Party Limited)

Lobel, Arnold. *Frog and Toad All Year.* Harper & Row, 1976. (Canada & UK: HarperCollins Pub. Ltd.; AUS: HarperCollins)

————*Frog and Toad Are Friends.* Harper & Row, 1970. (Canada & UK: HarperCollins Pub. Ltd.; AUS: HarperCollins)

————*Mouse Soup.* Harper & Row, 1977. (Canada & UK: HarperCollins Pub. Ltd.; AUS: HarperCollins)

————*Owl at Home.* Harper & Row, 1975. (Canada & UK: HarperCollins Pub. Ltd.; AUS: HarperCollins)

Lopshire, Robert. *The Biggest, Smallest, Fastest, Tallest Things You've Ever Heard Of.* Houghton Mifflin, 1961. (Canada: Thomas Allen & Son; UK: Cassell; AUS: Jackaranda Wiley)

Lord, John Vernon. *The Giant Jam Sandwich.* Houghton, 1973. (Canada: Thomas Allen & Son; UK: Cassell; AUS: Jackaranda Wiley)

MacLachlan, Patricia. *Mama One, Mama Two.* The Trumpet Club, 1982. (Canada & UK: HarperCollins Publishers Ltd.; AUS: HarperCollins)

————*Sarah, Plain and Tall.* New York: HarperCollins, 1985. (Canada & UK: HarperCollins Pub. Ltd.; AUS: HarperCollins)

Magorian, Michelle. *Who's Going to Take Care of Me?* HarperCollins, 1990. (Canada & UK: HarperCollins Pub. Ltd.; AUS: HarperCollins)

Marcus, Elizabeth. *Amazing World of Plants.* Troll, 1984. (Canada: Vanwell Pub.; UK & AUS: Penguin)

————*Our Wonderful Seasons.* Troll, 1983. (Canada: Vanwell Pub.; UK & AUS: Penguin)

Marshall, James. *George and Martha Round and Round.* Houghton Mifflin, 1988. (Canada: Thomas Allen & Son; UK: Cassell; AUS: Jackaranda Wiley)

Martin, Bill Jr. and John Archambault. *Barn Dance!* Henry Holt and Company, 1986. (Canada: Fitz Henry & Whiteside; UK: Pan Demic; Limited; AUS: CIS Publishers)

————*Chicka Chicka Boom Boom.* Scholastic, 1989. (Canada: Scholastic; UK: Scholastic Limited; AUS: Ashton Scholastic Party Limited)

Children's Literature References (cont.)

Martin, Jerome. *Mitten/Kitten*. Simon and Schuster, 1991. (Canada: Distican; UK: Simon & Schuster; AUS: Prentice Hall)

Martin, Patricia Stone. *Christa McAuliffe: Reaching for the Stars*. Rourke Enterprises, 1987.

Matthews, Morgan. *Which Way Hugo?* Troll Associates, 1986. (Canada: Vanwell Pub.; UK & AUS: Penguin)

Mayer, Mercer. *Frog Goes to Dinner*. Dial Books for Young Readers, 1974. (Canada: Penguin Bks Can; UK: Penguin UK; AUS: Penguin Bks AUS)

————*Frog on His Own*. Dial Books for Young Readers, 1973. (Canada: Penguin Bks Can; UK: Penguin UK; AUS: Penguin Bks AUS)

————*Frog, Where Are You?* Dial Press, 1969. (Canada: Penguin Bks Can; UK: Penguin UK; AUS: Penguin Bks AUS)

Mayer, Mercer and Marianna. *A Boy, a Dog, a Frog and a Friend*. Dial Books for Young Readers, 1971. (Canada: Penguin Bks Can; UK: Penguin UK; AUS: Penguin Bks AUS)

————*One Frog Too Many*. Dial Books for Young Readers, 1975. (Canada: Penguin Bks Can; UK: Penguin UK; AUS: Penguin Bks AUS)

Mayes, Susan. *What's Underground*. Usborne, 1989.

McGovern, Ann. *If You Lived in Colonial Times*. Scholastic, 1992. (Canada: Scholastic; UK: Scholastic Limited; AUS: Ashton Scholastic Party Limited)

McMillan, Bruce. *One Sun*. Scholastic, 1990. (Canada: Scholastic; UK: Scholastic Limited; AUS: Ashton Scholastic Party Limited)

Meltzer, Lisa. *The Elephant's Child*. Checkerboard Press, 1989. (Canada: General Pub.; UK: English House Services)

Metral, Yvette. *The Turtle*. Watermill Press, 1983. (Canada: Vanwell Pub.; UK & AUS: Penguin)

Milios, Rita. *I Am*. Children's Press, 1987. (Canada: Riverwood; AUS: Franklin Watts)

Milton, Joyce. *Christopher Columbus*. Scholastic, 1976. (Canada: Scholastic; UK: Scholastic Limited; AUS: Ashton Scholastic Party Limited)

————*Whales: the Gentle Giants*. Random House, 1989. (Canada & AUS: Random House; UK: Random Century House)

Moche, Dinah L. *My First Book About Space*. Western Publishing, 1982. (Canada & UK: Western Pub. Inc.; AUS: Golden Press Party Ltd.)

Mosel, Arlene. *Tikki Tikki Tembo*. Holt, Rinehart, and Winston, 1968. (Canada & UK: HBJ; AUS: HBJ AUS)

Most, Bernard. *Four and Twenty Dinosaurs*. The Trumpet Club, 1990. (Can & UK: HarperCollins Publishers Ltd.; AUS: HarperCollins)

————*There's an Ant in Anthony*. William Morrow and Company, 1980. (Canada: Gage Distributors; UK: International Book Distributors; AUS: Kirby Book Co.)

Munsch, Robert. *Jonathan Cleaned Up—Then He Heard a Sound*. Willowisp Press, 1980.

Myers, Bernice. *It Happens to Everyone*. Trumpet Club, 1990.

Nature Study Guild. *Master Flower Finder*. Warner Books, 1986.

Neasi, Barbara J. *Listen to Me*. Children's Press, 1986. (Canada: Riverwood; AUS: Franklin Watts)

Children's Literature References *(cont.)*

Numeroff, Laura Joffe. *If You Give a Mouse a Cookie.* Scholastic, 1985. (Canada: Scholastic; UK: Scholastic Limited; AUS: Ashton Scholastic Party Limited)

O'Keefe, Susan Heyboer. *One Hungry Monster: A Counting Book in Rhyme.* Scholastic Inc., 1989. (Canada: Scholastic; UK: Scholastic Limited; AUS: Ashton Scholastic Party Limited)

O'Neill, Catherine. *Let's Visit a Chocolate Factory.* Troll Associates, 1988. (Canada: Vanwell Pub.; UK & AUS: Penguin)

Oppenheim, Joanne. *Eency Weency Spider.* Bantam, 1991. (Canada: Doubleday Dell Seal; UK: Bantam Doubleday Dell; AUS: Transworld Pub.)

Oran, Hiawyn. *Angry Arthur.* The Trumpet Club, 1982. (Canada: Penguing Bks Can; AUS: Penguin Bks AUS; UK: Penguin UK)

Ormsby, Virginia H. *Twenty-One Children Plus Ten.* J.B. Lippincott, 1971. (UK: Peter Gemmel)

Pallotta, Jerry. *The Icky Bug Book.* Trumpet Club, 1986.

———*The Yucky Reptile Book.* Trumpet Club, 1989.

Parish, Peggy. *Amelia Bedelia Helps Out.* Avon Books, 1979. (Al Polan Intercontinental Book Distributors. 599 Industrial Ave., Paramus NJ 07652 (210) 967-5810)

———*Good Work, Amelia Bedelia.* Greenwillow Books, 1976. (Canada: Gage Distributors; UK: International Book Distributors; AUS: Kirby Book Co.)

———*Mind Your Manners.* Greenwillow Books, 1978. (Canada: Gage Distributors; UK: International Book Distributors; AUS: Kirby Book Co.)

Parsons, Alexandra. *Amazing Birds.* Alfred A. Knopf, 1990. (Canada: Penguin Books Can; UK: Dorling Kindersley; AUS: HarperCollins)

Peet, Bill. *The Wump World.* Houghton Mifflin, 1970. (Canada: Thomas Allen & Son; UK: Cassell; AUS: Jackaranda Wiley)

Perkins, Al. *Hand, Hand, Fingers, Thumb.* Random House, 1969. (Canada & AUS: Random House; UK: Random Century House)

Perrault, Charles. *Puss in Boots.* Farrar, Strauss and Giroux, 1990. (Canada: HarperCollins; UK: Victor Gollancz; AUS: Jackaranda Wiley)

Piper, Watty. *The Little Engine That Could.* Platt & Munk, 1990. (Canada: BeJo Sales; UK & AUS: Warner International)

Politi, Leo. *Song of the Swallows.* Macmillan, 1948. (Canada: Distican; UK: Simon & Schuster; AUS: Prentice Hall)

Pons, Helene. *The Story of Vania.* Viking Press, 1963. (Canada: Penguin Books Can; UK: Penguin UK; AUS: Penguin Books AUS)

Porter, Sue. *Little Wolf and the Giant.* Simon & Schuster, 1989. (Canada: Distican; UK: Simon & Schuster; AUS: Prentice Hall)

Poskanzer, Susan Cornell. *What's It Like to Be a Puppeteer?* Troll, 1989. (Canada: Vanwell Publishing; UK & AUS: Penguin)

Prager, Annabelle. *The Surprise Party.* Random House, 1988. (Canada & AUS: Random House; UK: Random Century House)

Prelutsky, Jack. *It's Valentine's Day.* Greenwillow Books, 1983. (Canada: Gage Distributors; UK: International Book Distributors; AUS: Kirby Book Co.)

Children's Literature References *(cont.)*

Prelutsky, Jack. *The New Kid on the Block*. Greenwillow, 1984. (Canada: Gage Distributors; UK: International Book Dist.; AUS: Kirby Book Co.)

————*Something BIG Has Been Here*. Scholastic, 1990. (Canada: Scholastic; UK: Scholastic Limited; AUS: Ashton Scholastic Party Limited)

Provensen, Alice and Martin. *The Year at Maple Hill Farm*. Atheneum, 1978. (Canada: Distican; UK: Simon & Schuster; AUS: Prentice Hall)

Pryor, Bonnie. *The House on Maple Street*. William Morrow and Company, Inc., 1987. (Canada: Gage Distributors; UK: International Book Dist.; AUS: Kirby Book Co.)

Rice, Elizabeth. *I'm Alvin*. Austin: Steck-Vaughn, 1967.

Richardson, James. *Science Dictionary of Animals*. Troll Associates, 1992. (Canada: Vanwell Pub.; UK & AUS: Penguin)

Rinkoff, Barbara. *A Map Is a Picture*. Thomas Y. Crowell, 1965. (Canada & UK: HarperCollins Pub. Ltd.; AUS: HarperCollins)

Rockwell, Anne & Harlow. *Happy Birthday to Me*. Field Publications, 1981. (Canada: Distican; UK: Simon & Schuster; AUS: Prentice Hall)

————*How My Garden Grew*. Field Publications, 1982. (Canada: Distican; UK: Simon & Schuster; AUS: Prentice Hall)

Rockwell, Harlow. *I Did It . . .* Macmillan Publishing, 1974. (Canada: Distican; UK: Simon & Schuster; AUS: Prentice Hall)

Rounds, Glen. *Wild Horses of the Red Desert*. Scholastic, 1971. (Canada: Scholastic; UK: Scholastic Limited; AUS: Ashton Scholastic Party Limited)

Rylant, Cynthia. *When I Was Young in the Mountains*. E.P. Dutton, 1982. (AUS: Penguin Books AUS; UK: Penguin)

Sabin, Francene. *Wonders of the Forest*. Troll, 1982. (Canada: Vanwell Pub.; UK & AUS: Penguin)

Sabin, Louis. *Television and Radio*. Troll Associates, 1985. (Canada: Vanwell Pub.; UK & AUS: Penguin)

Sapienza, Marilyn. *Stone Soup*. Weekly Reader Books, 1986.

Scholastic Editors. *My First Book of Words*. Scholastic, 1992. (Canada: Scholastic; UK: Scholastic Limited; AUS: Ashton Scholastic Party Limited)

Schweninger, Ann. *Valentine Friends*. Viking Kestrel, 1988. (Canada: Penguin Books Can; UK: Penguin UK; AUS: Penguin Books AUS)

Scieszka, Jon. *The True Story of the Three Little Pigs by A. Wolf*. Viking, 1989. (Canada: Penguin Books Can; UK: Penguin UK; AUS: Penguin Books AUS)

Selsam, Millicent E. *Seeds and More Seeds*. Harper & Row, 1959. (Canada & UK: HarperCollins Publisher Ltd.; AUS: HarperCollins)

Sedak: Maurice. *Where the Wild Things Are*. Harper & Row, 1963. (Canada & UK: HarperCollins Publisher Ltd.; AUS: HarperCollins)

Seuss, Dr. *The Cat in the Hat*. Random House, 1957. (Canada & AUS: Random House; UK: Random Century House)

————*The Cat in the Hat Comes Back*. Random House, 1958. (Canada & AUS: Random House; UK: Random Century House)

————*Dr. Seuss's ABC*. Random, 1963. (Canada & AUS: Random House; UK: Random Century House)

Children's Literature References *(cont.)*

Seuss, Dr. *Great Day for Up*. Random House, 1974. (Canada & AUS: Random House; UK: Random Century House)

————*Green Eggs and Ham*. Random House, 1960. (Canada & AUS: Random House; UK: Random Century House)

————*Hop on Pop*. Random House, 1963. (Canada & AUS: Random House; UK: Random Century House)

————*Mr. Brown Can Moo, Can You?* Random House, 1970. (Canada & AUS: Random House; UK: Random Century House)

————*One Fish, Two Fish, Red Fish, Blue Fish*. Random House, 1960. (Canada & AUS: Random House; UK: Random Century House)

————*There's a Wocket in My Pocket*. Random House, 1974. (Canada & AUS: Random House; UK: Random Century House)

Shannon, George. *Stories to Solve*. Trumpet Club, 1985. (Canada: Gage Distributors; UK: International Book. Dist.; AUS: Kirby Book Co.)

Sharmat, Marjorie Weinman. *A Big Fat Enormous Lie*. E.P. Dutton, 1978. (Canada: Penguin Bks Can; AUS: Penguin Books AUS; UK: Penguin)

Sharmat, Mitchell. *Gregory, the Terrible Eater*. Scholastic, 1980. (Canada: Scholastic; UK: Scholastic Limited; AUS: Ashton Scholastic Party Limited)

Shaw, Nancy. *Sheep in a Jeep*. Houghton Mifflin, 1986. (Canada: Thomas Allen & Son; UK: Cassell; AUS: Jackaranda Wiley)

————*Sheep in a Shop*. Houghton Mifflin, 1991. (Canada: Thomas Allen & Son; UK: Cassell; AUS: Jackaranda Wiley)

Showers, Paul. *The Listening Walk*. Thomas Y. Crowell, 1961. (Canada & UK: HarperCollins Pub. Ltd.; AUS: HarperCollins)

Silverstein, Shel. *The Giving Tree*. Harper & Row, 1964. (Canada & UK: HarperCollins Pub. Ltd.; AUS: HarperCollins)

————*Where the Sidewalk Ends*. Harper & Row, 1974. (Canada & UK: HarperCollins Pub. Ltd.; AUS: HarperCollins)

Simon, Seymour. *Stars*. Mulberry, 1986.

Slier, Debby (retold by). *The Brementown Musicians*. Checkerboard Press, 1989. (Canada: General Pub.; UK: English House Services;)

Slobodkina, Esphyr. *Caps for Sale*. Addison-Wesley, 1940.

Spier, Peter. *Noah's Ark*. Doubleday & Co., Inc., 1977. (Canada: Doubleday Dell Seal; UK: Bantam Doubleday Dell; AUS: Transworld Pub.)

————*Rain*. New York: Doubleday, 1982. (Canada: Doubleday Dell Seal; UK: Bantam Doubleday Dell; AUS: Transworld Pub.)

Steig, William. *Sylvester and the Magic Pebble*. Trumpet, 1969. (Canada: Distican; UK: Simon & Schuster; AUS: Prentice Hall)

Stevens, Carla. *Bear's Magic and Other Stories*. Scholastic, 1976. (Canada: Scholastic; UK: Scholastic Limited; AUS: Ashton Scholastic Party Ltd.)

Stevenson, Robert Louis. *My Shadow*. Trumpet Club, 1990. (Canada: BeJo Sales; UK & AUS: Warner International)

Supraner, Robyn. *No Room for a Sneeze*. Troll, 1986. (Canada: Vanwell Pub.; UK & AUS: Penguin)

Tafuri, Nancy. *Junglewalk*. Greenwillow Books, 1988. (Canada: Gage Distributors; UK: International Book Dist.; AUS: Kirby Book Co.)

Children's Literature References *(cont.)*

Terban, Marvin. *Eight Ate*. Clarion Books, 1982. (Canada: Thomas Allen & Son; UK: Cassell; AUS: Jackaranda Wiley)

————*In a Pickle and Other Funny Idioms*. Clarion Books, 1983. (Canada: Thomas Allen & Son; UK: Cassell; AUS: Jackaranda Wiley)

Tester, Sylvia Root. *Sometimes I'm Afraid*. Children's Press, 1939. (Canada: Riverwood; AUS: Franklin Watts)

Thaler, Mike. *A Hippopotamus Ate the Teacher*. Avon Books, 1981. (Al Polan Interconinental Book Distributors, 599 Industrial Ave Pramos, NJ 07652, (201) 967-5810)

Thomson, Ruth. *All About Sounds*. Gareth Stevens Publishing, 1989.

————*Trees*. E.D.C. Publishing, 1980.

Titus, Eve. *Anatole*. Bantam Books, 1956. (Canada: Doubleday Dell Seal; UK: Bantam Doubleday Dell; AUS: Transworld Pub.)

Tokuda, Wendy & Hall, Richard. *Humphrey the Lost Whale*. Heian International, 1986.

Tymms, Jean. *I Like to See—A Book About the Five Senses*. Western Publishing, 1973. (Canada & UK: Western Pub. Inc.; AUS: Golden Press Party Ltd.)

Udry, Janice May. *A Tree Is Nice*. Harper & Row, 1956. (Canada & UK: HarperCollins Publisher Ltd.; AUS: HarperCollins)

Ungerer, Tomi. *Crictor*. Harper & Row, 1958. (Canada & UK: HarperCollins Publisher Ltd.; AUS: HarperCollins)

Unkelbach, Kurt. *How to Train Your Puppy*. Reader's Digest Services.

Unwin, Nora S. *Proud Pumpkin*. Aladdin Books, 1953.

Van Allsburg, Chris. *Jumanji*. Houghton Mifflin, 1981. (Canada: Thomas Allen & Son; UK: Cassell; AUS: Jackaranda Wiley)

————*Just a Dream*. Houghton Mifflin, 1990. (Canada: Thomas Allen & Son; UK: Cassell; AUS: Jackaranda Wiley)

Viorst, Judith. *Alexander and the Terrible, Horrible, No Good, Very Bad Day*. Macmillan, 1972. (Canada: Distican; UK: Simon & Schuster; AUS: Prentice Hall)

Waber, Bernard. *An Anteater Named Arthur*. Houghton Mifflin Co., 1967. (Canada: Thomas Allen & Son; UK: Cassell; AUS: Jackaranda Wiley)

————*Ira Sleeps Over*. Houghton Mifflin, 1972. (Canada: Thomas Allen & Son; UK: Cassell; AUS: Jackaranda Wiley)

Wahl, Jan. *The Toy Circus*. Gulliver Books, 1986. (Canada & UK: HBJ; AUS: HBJ AUS)

Ward, Lynd. *The Biggest Bear*. Houghton Mifflin Co., 1952. (Canada: Thomas Allen & Son; UK: Cassell; AUS: Jackaranda Wiley)

Wasserman, Selma and Jack. *What's Alike? What's Different?* Walker and Company, 1990.

Watson, N. Cameron. *The Little Pigs Puppet Book*. Little, Brown & Co., 1990. (Canada: Little Brown; UK: Little Brown Ltd.; AUS: Penguin)

Watts, Mabel. *The Day It Rained Watermelons*. Lantern Press, 1964.

Werner, Sara. *The Long, Green Pencil*. Raintree Publishers, 1990. (Canada: Pippin; UK & AUS: Raintree)

Westcott, Nadine Bernard. *I Know an Old Lady Who Swallowed a Fly*. Little, Brown, and Co., 1980. (Canada: Little Brown; UK: Little Brown Ltd.; AUS: Penguin)

Children's Literature References *(cont.)*

Whitehead, Pat. *Best Thanksgiving Book: ABC Adventures.* Troll, 1985. (Canada: Vanwell Pub.; UK & AUS: Penguin)

Wiesner, David. *Free Fall.* Lothrop, Lee & Shepard Books, 1988. (Canada: Gage Distributors; UK: International Book Dist.; AUS: Kirby Book Co.)

Wilder, Laura Ingalls. *Little House in the Big Woods.* Scholastic, 1932. (Canada: Scholastic; UK: Scholastic Ltd.; AUS: Ashton Scholastic Party Ltd.)

Williams, Margery. *The Velveteen Rabbit.* Avon Books, 1975. Al Polan Intercontinental Book Distributors, 599 Industrial Ave. Pramus, NJ 07652, (201) 967-5810)

Willow, Diane. *At Home in the Rain Forest.* Charlesbridge, 1991. (All countries call (617) 926-0329)

Wilner, Isabel. *B Is for Bethlehem: A Christmas Alphabet.* Dutton Children's Books, 1990. (Canada: Penguin Bks Can; AUS: Penguin Bks. AUS; UK: Penguin)

Winter, Jeanette. *Follow the Drinking Gourd.* Trumpet, 1988. (Canada: Penguin Books Can; UK: Dorling Kindersley; AUS: HarperCollins)

Wiseman, Bernard. *Morris Has a Cold.* Dodd, Mead, & Co., 1978.

Wood, Audrey. *The Napping House.* Harcourt Brace Jovanovich, 1984. (Canada & UK: HBJ; AUS: HBJ AUS)

Wylie, Joanne and David. *A Big Fish Story.* Regensteiner Publishing Enterprises, Inc., 1983. (Canada: Riverwood; AUS: Franklin Watts)

Yabuuchi, Masayuki. *Animals Sleeping.* Philomel Books, 1981. (Canada: BeJo Sales; UK & AUS: Warner International)

————*Whose Baby.* Philomel Books, 1985. (Canada: BeJo Sales; UK & AUS: Warner International)

————*Whose Footprints?* Philomel Books, 1985. (Canada: BeJo Sales; UK & AUS: Warner International)

Yektai, Niki. *Hi Bears, Bye Bears.* Orchard Books, 1990. (Canada: Gage Distributors; UK: Baker & Taylor International; AUS: Franklin Watts AUS)

Yorinks, Arthur. *Hey Al.* HarperCollins Publishers, 1986. (Canada: HarperCollins; UK: Victor Gollancz; AUS: Jackaranda Wiley)

Yoshi. *Who's Hiding Here?* Natick Picture Book Studio, 1987. (Canada: Distican; UK: Simon & Schuster; AUS: Prentice Hall)

Young, Ed. *Lon Po Po.* Scholastic, 1989. (Canada: Scholastic; UK: Scholastic Ltd.; AUS: Ashton Scholastic Party Ltd.)

Zion, Gene. *Harry the Dirty Dog.* HarperCollins, 1956. (Canada & UK: HarperCollins Pub. Ltd.; AUS: HarperCollins)

Zolotow, Charlotte. *Over and Over.* Harper & Row, 1957. (Canada & UK: HarperCollins Pub. Ltd.; AUS: HarperCollins)

————*Mr. Rabbit and the Lovely Present.* HarperCollins, 1962. (Canada & UK: HarperCollins Pub. Ltd.; AUS: HarperCollins)

————*The Storm Book: U.S.A.*: Harper & Row, 1952. (Canada & UK: HarperCollins Pub. Ltd.; AUS: HarperCollins)